# Singleton

The Singleton design pattern ensures that not more than one instance of a class is created and provides a global point of access to this instance.

# Iterator

The Iterator design pattern provides a uniform way of traversing the elements of a collection object.

# Adapter

The Adapter design pattern is useful in situations where an existing class provides a needed service but there is a mismatch between the interface offered and the interface clients expect. The Adapter pattern shows how to convert the interface of the existing class into the interface clients expect.

# Decorator

The decorator design pattern provides a way of attaching additional responsibilities to an object dynamically. It uses object composition rather than class inheritance for a lightweight flexible approach to adding responsibilities to objects at runtime.

# State

If an object goes through clearly identifiable states, and the object's behavior is especially dependent on its state, it is a good candidate for the State design pattern.

# Strategy

The Strategy design pattern defines a family of algorithms, encapsulates each one, and makes them interchangeable. Strategy lets the algorithm vary independently from clients that use it (Gamma, et al. 1995).

# Factory Method

The Factory Method Pattern "defines an interface for creating an object, but lets subclasses decide which class to instantiate. Factory Method lets a class defer instantiation to subclasses" (Gamma, et al. 1995).

## Observer

The Observer design pattern defines a one-to-many relationship between a subject object and any number of observer objects such that when the subject object changes, observer objects are notified and given a chance to react to changes in the subject.

## Façade

The intent of the Façade design pattern is to "provide a unified interface to a set of interfaces in a subsystem. Facade defines a higher-level interface that makes the subsystem easier to use" (Gamma, et al. 1995).

*return to pg 4 after reading about facade*

## Template Method

With the Template Method design pattern the structure of an algorithm is represented once with variations on the algorithm implemented by subclasses. The skeleton of the algorithm is declared in a template method in terms of overridable operations. Subclasses are allowed to extend or replace some or all of these operations.

# Programming in the Large with Design Patterns

Eddie Burris

**Publisher:** Pretty Print Press, Leawood Kansas 66209.

**Version History**

April 2012  -  Initial release.

June 2012  -  Fixed problem with image resolution and corrected errors in Factory Method sample code.

July 2012  -  First print edition. Added an index and proper references.

# Contents

Preface...................................................................................................ix

Chapter 1  Introduction to Design Patterns ...................................1

    History of Design Patterns...............................................................4

    What is a Software Design Pattern? ...............................................8

    Reverse Engineering a Design Pattern..........................................11

    Pattern Categories..........................................................................14

    A Few Non-Patterns .......................................................................19

    Benefits of Design Patterns ............................................................19

    Intent Matters.................................................................................22

    Design Pattern Templates ..............................................................23

    Introduction to the Patterns...........................................................24

Chapter 2  Singleton........................................................................25

    Introduction....................................................................................25

    Intent..............................................................................................26

    Solution..........................................................................................26

    Sample Code ..................................................................................28

    Discussion......................................................................................29

    Related Patterns .............................................................................33

Chapter 3  Iterator ..........................................................................35

    Introduction....................................................................................35

    Intent..............................................................................................36

    Solution..........................................................................................36

    Sample Code ..................................................................................43

    Discussion......................................................................................44

    Related Patterns .............................................................................46

Chapter 4  Adapter ..........................................................................47

    Introduction....................................................................................47

Intent .................................................................................................. 52

Solution ............................................................................................. 52

Sample Code ..................................................................................... 57

Discussion .......................................................................................... 59

Related Patterns ................................................................................ 60

Chapter 5  Decorator .......................................................................... 63

Introduction ...................................................................................... 63

Intent .................................................................................................. 67

Solution ............................................................................................. 67

Sample Code ..................................................................................... 70

Discussion .......................................................................................... 72

Related Patterns ................................................................................ 74

Chapter 6  State ................................................................................... 75

Introduction ...................................................................................... 75

Intent .................................................................................................. 76

Solution ............................................................................................. 76

Sample Code ..................................................................................... 77

Discussion .......................................................................................... 83

Related Patterns ................................................................................ 83

Chapter 7  Strategy ............................................................................. 85

Introduction ...................................................................................... 85

Intent .................................................................................................. 86

Solution ............................................................................................. 87

Sample Code ..................................................................................... 88

Discussion .......................................................................................... 91

Related Patterns ................................................................................ 92

Chapter 8  Factory Method ................................................................ 93

Introduction ...................................................................................... 93

Intent .................................................................................................. 95

Solution.................................................................97

Sample Code........................................................98

Discussion..........................................................102

Related Patterns ................................................104

Chapter 9  Observer ..........................................107

Introduction......................................................107

Intent.................................................................108

Solution............................................................108

Sample Code.....................................................111

Discussion.........................................................114

Related Patterns ................................................116

Chapter 10  Façade.............................................117

Introduction......................................................117

Intent.................................................................119

Solution............................................................119

Sample Code.....................................................120

Discussion.........................................................124

Related Patterns ................................................125

Chapter 11  Template Method.............................127

Introduction......................................................127

Intent.................................................................129

Solution............................................................130

Sample Code.....................................................131

Discussion.........................................................134

Related Patterns ................................................137

Bibliography........................................................139

Index ...................................................................141

# Preface

For several years I ran a web site that offered educational materials on a variety of software engineering topics. The most popular search term at the site by a considerable margin was "design patterns". Design patterns have captured the attention of the developer community, and for good reason.

In a word, the reason is *design*. Good design is critical to the long-term success of nontrivial computer programs. Companies are willing to pay top dollar for talented designers and architects that can deliver software that is testable, extensible and free from unnecessary complexity.

One option for acquiring the expertise needed to be an effective designer is to spend 10-15 years working as a designer or as an apprentice to a designer. Learning from first-hand experience has many advantages but the one big disadvantage is the time it takes to acquire the knowledge. It can take a decade or more to experience a broad range of design problems and even longer to experience similar problems in different contexts. Another more efficient route to becoming a skilled designer is to study design patterns. Design patterns capture expert knowledge in a form that facilitates learning and reuse.

This book makes learning design patterns easy. It starts with a general introduction to all types of programming patterns and goes on to describe 10 of the most popular design patterns in detail: Singleton, Iterator, Adapter, Decorator, State, Strategy, Factory Method, Observer, Facade and Template Method.

Each pattern is introduced with a non-technical example or story that illustrates the pattern concept. The details are described with Java code examples and UML diagrams. Each pattern description also includes a discussion section that offers more in-depth information for the curious.

Instructor resources, including PowerPoint presentation slides and review questions with answers, are available at the companion website http://programminglarge.com/.

Eddie Burris
Leawood, Kansas

UML = Unified modeling language

# Chapter 1  Introduction to Design Patterns

Imagine you are in the late stages of designing a library automation system. The requirements call for a system that will allow a library patron to:

1.  Check out a book
2.  Return a book
3.  Renew a book, and
4.  Place a book on reserve

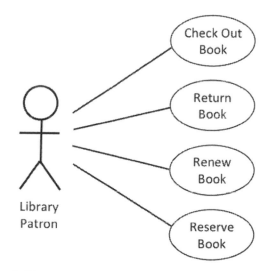

**Figure 1  Use case diagram for library automation system**

After a few iterations of original design you decide on the following 3 classes for the business logic:

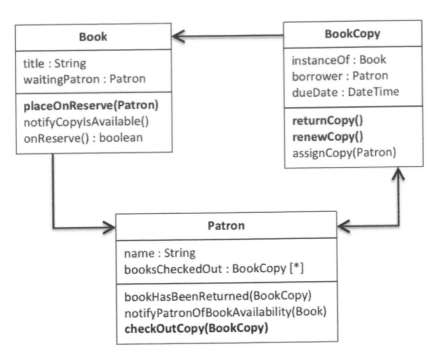

**Figure 2  Class diagram for library automation system**

It's a workable design but not a great design. It addresses all the requirements, but the main features (shown in bold in Figure 2) are distributed over three classes. The user interface (UI) subsystem that will make use of the features will have dependencies on all three classes. The coupling between the UI subsystem and core logic could be reduced if all features were accessible from a single component.

How would you go about solving this design problem?

If you fancy yourself an engineer, your first inclination should be to look for a routine or existing design solution before resorting to original design. For software engineers this means consulting handbooks on design patterns. Luckily you are holding one in your hand right now. Read through the design pattern digest at the front of this book to see if any of the patterns might offer a solution to the current design problem.

Reading through the design pattern summaries at the front of this book, there is one that stands out:

> **Façade**—The intent of the Façade design pattern is to "provide a unified interface to a set of interfaces in a subsystem. Facade defines a higher-level interface that makes the subsystem easier to use" (Gamma, et al. 1995).

Façade seems to be a good match for the problem at hand. The full write-up for the pattern in chapter 10 provides guidelines for applying the pattern in different contexts. The result after applying it to the current design problem would look something like:

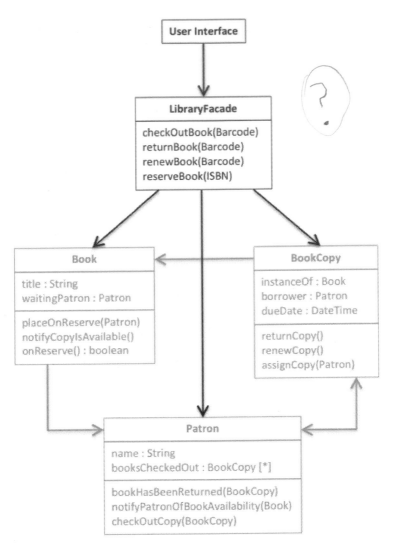

**Figure 3  Unified interface onto library automation subsystem**

In this example, high coupling signaled a weakness in the design, which was then remedied with the Façade design pattern. Design will always involve some level of creativity and innovation but skillful application of design principles and patterns can help make the process a little more routine.

## History of Design Patterns

Design patterns are reusable solutions to reoccurring design problems. The idea of designing with patterns didn't start with software though; it started in the realm of urban planning and building architecture. In the 1970's, Christopher Alexander set out to create a pattern language that ordinary people could use to create more enjoyable buildings and public spaces. The first book on patterns, *A Pattern Language: Towns, Buildings, Construction*, documented 253 such patterns. Each pattern provided a general solution to a reoccurring design problem in a particular context.

For another perspective on how patterns work in general, consider Low Sill, a pattern proposed by Christopher Alexander for determining the height of a windowsill. Here is a summary of the pattern in standard form (Alexander, et al., 1977):

**Context**: Windows are being planned for a wall.

**Problem**: How high should the windowsill be from the floor? A windowsill that is too high cuts you off from the outside world. One that is too low could be mistaken for a door and is potentially unsafe.

**Solution**: Design the windowsill to be 12 to 14 inches from the floor. On upper floors, for safety, make them higher, around 20 inches. The primary function of a window is to connect building occupants to the outside world. The link is more meaningful when both the ground and horizon are visible when standing a foot or two away from the window.

**Figure 4  Low windowsill (Photo credit: Searl Lamaster Howe Architects)**

This example illustrates a couple of important characteristics of patterns. First, design (and more generally engineering) is about balancing conflicting forces or constraints. Here the objective is to make the windowsill low enough to see the ground in order to make a connection with the outside world but high enough to be safe and not to be confused with a door.

Second, design patterns provide general solutions at a medium level of abstraction. They don't give exact answers (precise measurements in the case of Low Sill), and at the same time, they are more concrete and practical than abstract principles or strategies. In the example above, the solution is given in terms of a range of heights: 12 to 20 inches. How high to set a window will depend on preferences and local conditions. The optimal height is the value that best balances the conflicting forces.

Finally, patterns aren't dogma. The pattern doesn't say that *all* windowsills must be 12 to 20 inches off the floor. If you are designing a jail cell, for example, there may be overriding factors that call for a windowsill higher than the recommended 12 to 20 inches.

Ten years after the publication of Christopher Alexander's book on architectural patterns, Kent Beck and Ward Cunningham proposed creating a pattern language for software design analogous to Christopher Alexander's pattern language for town and building design (Beck and Cunningham 1987). In support of their suggestion, they gave a brief experience report on 5 patterns they created for user interface design.

Just as Christopher Alexander envisioned ordinary citizens using architectural patterns to design and build the personal spaces they would occupy, Kent Beck and Ward Cunningham envisioned software design patterns empowering computer users to "write their own programs" (Smith 1987).

> Our initial success using a pattern language for user interface design has left us quite enthusiastic about the possibilities for computer users designing and programming their own applications (Smith 1987).

Neither collection of patterns has made significant inroads with end users, but both have been quite successful at documenting design knowledge in a way that makes it accessible and reusable—if only for professionals in the domain.

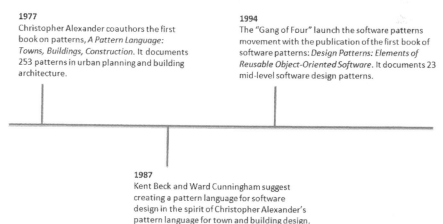

**1977**
Christopher Alexander coauthors the first book on patterns, *A Pattern Language: Towns, Buildings, Construction*. It documents 253 patterns in urban planning and building architecture.

**1994**
The "Gang of Four" launch the software patterns movement with the publication of the first book of software patterns: *Design Patterns: Elements of Reusable Object-Oriented Software*. It documents 23 mid-level software design patterns.

**1987**
Kent Beck and Ward Cunningham suggest creating a pattern language for software design in the spirit of Christopher Alexander's pattern language for town and building design.

**Figure 5  Important milestones in the history of design patterns**

The software patterns movement began in earnest after the publication of *Design Patterns: Elements of Reusable Object-Oriented Software*

(Gamma, et al. 1995). The four authors Erich Gamma, Richard Helm, Ralph Johnson and John Vlissides are collectively known as the "Gang of Four" or GofF. Many of the patterns in this book are widely accepted in the development community and therefore required knowledge for software development professionals.

## What is a Software Design Pattern?

A software design pattern is a reusable solution to a reoccurring software design problem. (For the rest of this chapter, assume the term design pattern refers to a *software* design pattern.) A design pattern is not a concrete design or implementation, such as an algorithm that can be used as-is, but rather a generic solution that must be adapted to the specific needs of the problem at hand.

To better understand what a design pattern is, recall the process and product of design. The purpose of the design process is to determine how the eventual code will be structured or organized into modules. The output of the design process is an abstract solution model typically expressed with a symbolic modeling language such as UML.

*Design pattern = generic solution that must be adapted to the specific needs of the problem at hand.*

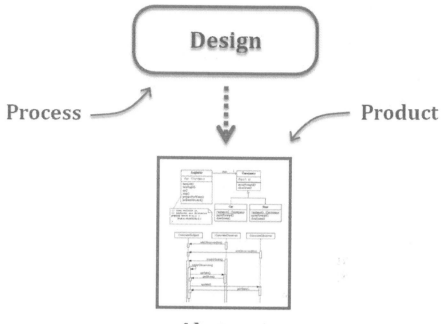

## Abstract
## Solution Model

**Figure 6  The output of the design process is an abstract solution model**

Design is probably the most challenging activity in the software development life cycle. There is no algorithm for deriving abstract solution models from requirements. The best the discipline of software engineering can offer are methods, techniques, heuristics, and the subject of this book, design patterns.

A design pattern is problem-solution pair. A design pattern provides a mapping from a specific design problem to a generic solution.

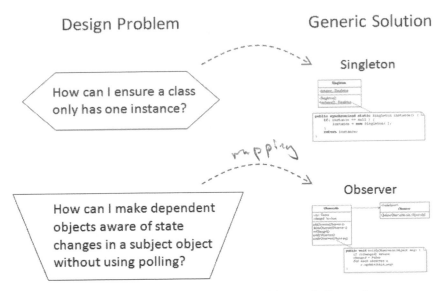

**Figure 7  A design pattern is a problem-solution pair**

Knowledge of design patterns simplifies software design by reducing the number of design problems that have to be solved from first principles. Design problems that match documented design patterns have ready-made solutions. The remaining problems that don't match documented design patterns must be solved from first principles. Even here, knowledge of design patterns can potentially help with original design. Design patterns are paragons of good design. Studying design patterns helps to develop the intellectual concepts and principles needed to solve unique design problems from first principles.

*Knowing already created design patterns helps original design easier because you have a good starting point.*

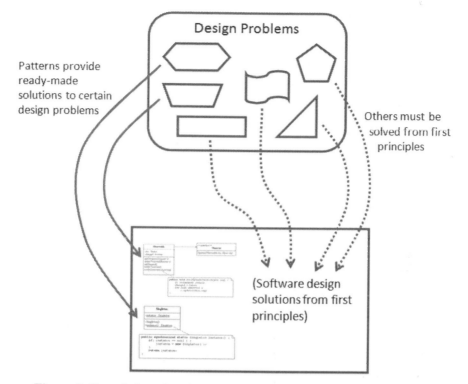

**Figure 8  Knowledge of design patterns reduces the number of design problems that have to be solved from first principles**

# Reverse Engineering a Design Pattern

A design pattern, and more generally a design, is an abstraction of an implementation. Because the human mind is better at forming abstractions from details, maybe the best way to get a deeper understanding of design patterns is to reverse engineer one from implementation. In this example I will extract the design from two code samples and then present the design pattern that corresponds to the design.

The following will be familiar to anyone who has written a GUI program in Java:

```
public class MyForm extends JFrame implements ActionListener
{
    public MyForm() {
        JButton b = new JButton();
        b.addActionListener(this);
    }

    public void actionPerformed(ActionEvent evt)
    {
        . . .
    }
}
```

**Figure 9  Event handling in Java**

Likewise, the following will be familiar to anyone who has written a GUI program in C#:

```
public class MyForm : Form
{
    public MyForm() {
        Button b = new Button();
        b.Click += new EventHandler(onClick);
    }

    public void onClick(object sender, System.EventArgs e)
    {
        . . .
    }
}
```

**Figure 10  Event handling in C#**

In each case an event handler or callback routine is registered to handle button click events. When the user clicks on the visible button, control passes to the registered event handler. Each implementation is unique, but in both cases the design is the same. In both cases the general design problem is how to allow one or more objects (those containing the event handling routines) to be notified when the state of another object (the button) changes. This is a routine design problem for which there exists a reusable solution in the form of the Observer design pattern.

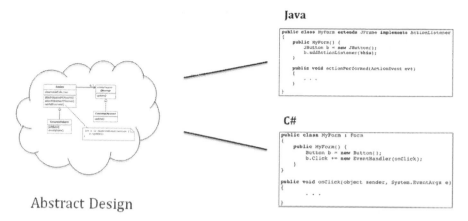

**Java**

```
public class MyForm extends JFrame implements ActionListener
{
    public MyForm() {
        JButton b = new JButton();
        b.addActionListener(this);
    }

    public void actionPerformed(ActionEvent evt)
    {
        . . .
    }
}
```

**C#**

```
public class MyForm : Form
{
    public MyForm() {
        Button b = new Button();
        b.Click += new EventHandler(onClick);
    }
}

public void onClick(object sender, System.EventArgs e)
{
    . . .
}
```

Abstract Design

Concrete Implementations

**Figure 11  Two implementations for the same abstract design**

The observer design pattern will be discussed in greater detail in chapter 9, but to give you some idea what a design pattern looks like, here is the Observer design pattern in outline form:

**Pattern Name**: Observer.

**Context**: One or more objects (observers) need to be made aware of state changes in another object (the subject).

**Problem**: The objects doing the observing (observers) should be decoupled from the object under observation (the subject). It should be possible to evolve and reuse subjects or observers independently of each other.

The subject shouldn't depend on the details of its observers. (The design complies with the dependency inversion principle.) Adding another observer shouldn't require a change to the subject.

**Solution**: Define a class or interface `Subject` with methods for attaching and detaching observers as well as a method for notifying attached observers when the state of the subject changes. Define an interface `Observer` that defines a callback method subjects can use to notify observers of a change.

Because natural language is not well suited to conveying design ideas (admit it, your eyes glazed over while reading the preceding paragraph), design patterns are often expressed using a visual modeling language such as UML. The following UML diagram shows the abstract solution model for the Observer design pattern.

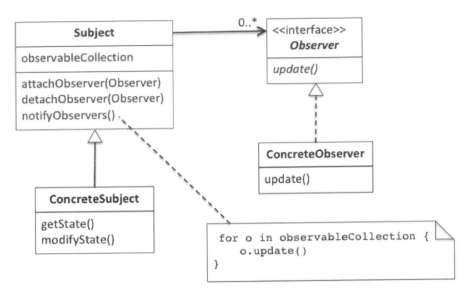

**Figure 12  Abstract solution model for Observer design pattern**

In this example, for pedagogical reasons, the code came before the design. In practice, you would of course discover the opportunity to use the Observer design pattern during design and then use the design pattern to derive the code.

## Pattern Categories

It's hard to keep a good idea from spreading. The use of patterns has branched out from design to find application in other stages of the software life cycle. Software patterns can be classified according to the development stage during which they are used: analysis, design and implementation. Patterns of design can further be distinguished by level of abstraction: high-level and mid-level. As Figure 13 shows, the four main categories of software patterns are: analysis patterns, architectural patterns, design patterns and programming idioms.

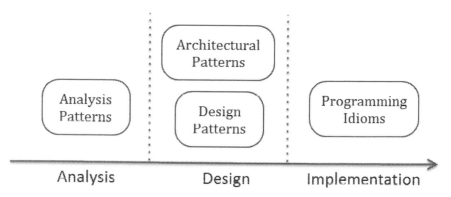

**Figure 13  Patterns throughout the software life cycle**

*Analysis Patterns*. Understanding the problem domain is an important part of the requirements process. This involves looking beyond the surface requirements in order to gain a deeper understanding of the underlying concepts in the problem domain. To illustrate, here is an example of concept discovery during the course of requirements elicitation:

> **User**: "We need to send out invoices."
>
> **Requirements Analyst**: "I assume you send these invoices to other companies."
>
> **User**: "Yes, that is correct…um, most of the time. Actually, some of the time we send them out to private individuals."
>
> **Requirements Analyst**: "So, the recipient of an invoice could be a company or an individual."
>
> **User**: "Yes, and government agencies too. They are like companies but are handled slightly differently."

What is slowly emerging here is the concept of responsible party. It is one of many concepts that experienced analysts know to look for when doing domain analysis or business modeling.

Just as design patterns document collective knowledge of common designs, analysis patterns document collective knowledge of common abstractions found in business modeling.

Figure 14 shows what the Responsible Party analysis pattern might look like in a domain model.

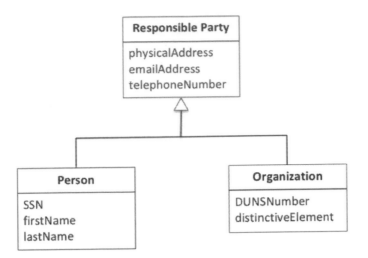

**Figure 14  UML diagram for the Responsible Party analysis pattern**

The UML analysis model in Figure 14 could easily be mistaken for a design. It is an analysis model by virtue of how it is used. The motivation for using analysis patterns is the desire to better understand the problem domain. However, because analysis models make excellent first-draft design models, it is not unusual for analysis models to evolve into design models, sometime with little or no modification.

The best reference for analysis patterns is Martin Fowler's book, *Analysis Patterns* (Fowler 1997). It documents 76 analysis patterns including Party and other familiar domain concepts such as Account, Contract, Product, Measurement and Quantity.

*Architectural Patterns*. Design occurs at different levels. The scale of the components of interest distinguishes the levels. At the architectural level, components are programs and subsystems. For mid-level design, components are classes and objects.

An architectural pattern is a high-level plan for organizing the top-level components of a program or software system.

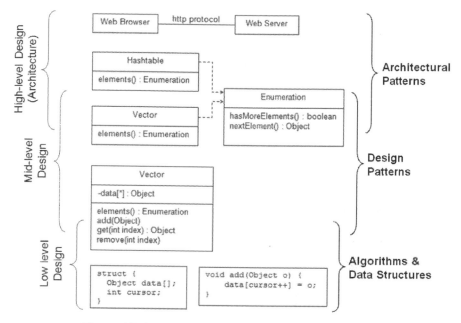

**Figure 15  Scope of architecture and design patterns**

Well-known architectural patterns (or styles) include: client-server, n-tiered, blackboard, and model-view controller (Buschmann, et al. 1996) (Shaw and Garlan 1996).

***Design Patterns***. As Figure 15 illustrates, design patterns address mid-level design problems. The solutions to these problems are defined by a small number of classes and/or objects. Design patterns are the subject of this book.

***Programming Idioms***. A programming idiom is a low-level, language-specific pattern that explains how to accomplish a simple task using a specific programming language or technology. For example, the following C++ idiom explains how to prevent objects in a C++ program from being copied (Coplien 1992).

> **Context**: In C++, objects are copied when passed by value or assigned. The design of a class may be such that copying an instance of the class would violate the semantics of the class. (For example, making a copy of an instance of a class that encapsulates a network connection would lead to chaos if both instances of the class were used interchangeably.)

> **Problem**: How to ensure instances of a C++ class are never copied?

**Solution**: Declare the copy-constructor and copy assignment operator of the class private and don't implement them. This makes them inaccessible outside the class. If you inadvertently write code that implicitly invokes one of these operations, you will get a link error.

```
class C
{
    . . .

    private:
        // There is no implementation for the
        // following two member functions
        C (const C&);
        C& operator= (const C&);
}
```

**Figure 16  C++ programming idiom**

A more popular term for programming idiom today is recipe. Just about every major programming language and platform technology has at least one "cookbook" of recipes for how to accomplish specific tasks using the language or platform (Martelli, et al. 2005) (Margolis 2011) (C. Fowler 2012).

Recipe is a good metaphor because the solutions given are precise step-by-step instructions. The amount of adaptation needed when applying a programming idiom is much less than what is needed when applying a design or architectural pattern.

Another point of distinction between programming idioms and design patterns relates to naming and the existence (or nonexistence) of a vocabulary. Most programming idioms have long awkward names that are a poor basis from which to build a vocabulary. Consider the following representative names: "Trimming space from the ends of a string", "Adding to or subtracting from a date", and "Generating URLs dynamically". Architectural and design pattern names simplify communication. A lot of information is communicated with a statement like: "I'm using the 3-tiered architectural pattern with Row Data Gateway in the data abstraction layer." It's hard to imagine names for programming idioms being used in the same way.

# A Few Non-Patterns

Not all problem-solution pairs are patterns. If the concept of a pattern is applied too loosely, it could dilute what it means to be a pattern. Although there is no formal criteria or litmus test for what is and isn't a pattern, there are a few problem-solution pairs that are not generally thought of as patterns.

**Algorithms are not design patterns**. Algorithms are not design patterns mainly because they have different objectives. The purpose of an algorithm is to solve a specific problem (sorting, searching, etc.) in a computationally efficient way as measured in terms of time and space complexity. The purpose of a design pattern is to organize code in a developmentally efficient way as measured in terms of flexibility, maintainability, reusability, etc.

Algorithms are not design patterns, but some might qualify as programming idioms. A simple algorithm specific to a programming language could be considered a programming idiom.

**One-off designs are not patterns**. Not every software design rises to the level of a pattern. Patterns are often described as reusable and well-proven solutions. You can't be sure a one-off design is reusable or well proven. The general rule-of-thumb is a software design can't be considered a pattern until it has been applied in a real-world solution at least three times (the so called "Rule of Three"). This is why many say that design patterns are discovered rather than invented.

# Benefits of Design Patterns

Design patterns generate a lot of interest in the development community. Here are some of the reasons why.

**Design patterns facilitate reuse**. The most common form of reuse in software development is code reuse. Libraries of reusable components (routines, classes, packages) are made available to programmers for integration (linking) into their applications.

Design patterns enable another form of reuse—design reuse. Practicing design reuse means looking for a routine design before resorting to the creation of an original design.

At design time there are certain design problems that have to be solved such as how to ensure not more than one instance of a class is created or how to attach responsibilities to an object at runtime. When faced with a design problem, designers can search catalogs of design patterns for an existing solution that meets their needs. What is being reused is the structure or organization of the code.

It's important to note that the solution provided is a design and not code. The design pattern may include sample code, but the purpose of the sample code is to illustrate the design not to be used as is without modification.

**Design patterns make design easier**. Design patterns make design easier but not *easy*. Their application still requires a modest amount of reasoning and problem solving.

First, before you can begin to apply design patterns you have to formulate the design problem. Problems solved by mid-level design patterns don't normally show up directly in a requirements document. Requirements are written from the perspective of the problem domain. Design patterns solve problems that arise in the context of the solution domain. Problems solved by mid-level design patterns don't start to show up until you begin to conceptualize solution structures. At best, written requirements might point the way to an architectural pattern (Requirements: *"the system shall display inventory data along with controls for updating the data"*. You: *"hum, seems like a problem suited to the Model-View-Controller architectural style"*).

Second, once you have identified a design problem you must be familiar enough with existing patterns to recognize the problem is one for which a design pattern exists. The pattern summaries included with many pattern books (and at the front of this book) can help with the search for a design pattern that addresses a specific design problem (Gamma, et al. 1995) (Buschmann, et al. 1996).

And finally, once identified, it takes skill to adapt the general pattern to fit the problem at hand. Applying design patterns is easier than solving design problems from first principles but their application still requires thoughtful decision making.

**Design patterns capture expertise and facilitate its dissemination**. Knowledge of design patterns can put you on the fast track to becoming an expert at design. Design patterns capture the body of knowledge that defines our understanding of good design in a way that makes it possible for others to learn from and reuse this knowledge. Experience is still important but design patterns are one of the most effective mechanisms for documenting and transferring design skill and knowledge from one analyst to another.

**Design patterns define a shared vocabulary for discussing design and architecture**. A common shared vocabulary is necessary for communication. The words in the vocabulary should also be at the appropriate level of abstract for the ideas being communicated. Catalogs of design patterns define a shared vocabulary at the right level of abstraction for efficient communication of design ideas. If one developer says to another "the data is connected to the user interface using the adapter pattern", the other developer has an understanding of a portion of the design, which includes substantial detail on code structure, intent, characteristics and constraints.

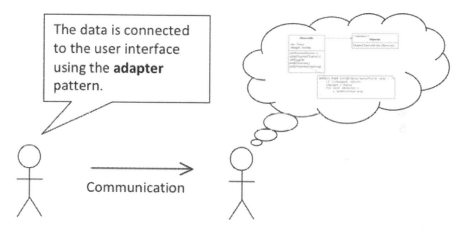

The data is connected to the user interface using the **adapter** pattern.

Communication

**Figure 17  Design patterns provide a vocabulary for discussing design**

To the extent that thought is influence by vocabulary (i.e. linguistic determinism), having a high-level vocabulary for discussing design makes it easier to reason about design and architecture. Thinking in terms of low-level artifacts such as declarations and control-flow structures may inhibit design insights and innovations.

**Design patterns move software development closer to a well-established engineering discipline**. Engineers look for routine solutions before resorting to original problem solving. A prime resource for the data and information engineers need to solve reoccurring problems are engineering handbooks. All established branches of engineering have well-known handbooks that offer practical information for solving reoccurring problems.

Handbooks of design patterns are important references for practicing software engineers. (Software engineers may also want to keep a handbook on refactoring close by when programming.) Having handbooks of reusable solutions to reoccurring design problems moves software engineering a step closer to becoming a well-established engineering discipline.

**Studying design patterns improves your ability to do original design.**
To be an effective designer you must have a solid understanding of
fundamental design concepts and principles such as coupling, information
hiding and the Open-Closed Principle. These abstract ideas can be difficult
(if not impossible) to fully appreciate without experiencing them in
context. Design patterns are a natural habitat for design concepts and
principles of good design. As you study design patterns your understanding
of these concepts and principles and your ability to apply them are likely to
improve even if you don't use the patterns directly.

**Knowing popular design patterns makes it easier to learn class
libraries that use design patterns**. Design patterns are common in
programming language class libraries and occasionally show up in the
language definition itself (e.g. the `foreach` statement in PHP is a
language implementation of the iterator design pattern). Learning a class
library is easier if you are familiar with the design patterns used in the
library. For example, the classes and interfaces that make up the Java IO
package are confusing to many new Java programmers simply because
they aren't familiar with the decorator design pattern. Programmers that
know the decorator design pattern quickly grasp how specific classes in the
Java IO package work and know what other types of classes to look for.

## Intent Matters

Those new to design patterns are often surprised to learn that design
patterns aren't distinguished by their static structure alone. To illustrate, try
taking the following design pattern blind comparison test.

Figure 18 shows two class diagrams, one is for the State design pattern
and the other is for the Strategy design pattern. Generic names for classes
and other identifiers have been used in order to avoid identifying marks
that would give away the answer. Can you tell which is which?

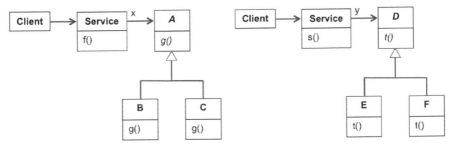

**Figure 18  Design pattern blind comparison test**

It is of course impossible to tell which diagram represents the State design pattern and which represents Strategy. Structurally they are identical.

What makes a design pattern unique is its intent. The intent of a pattern is the problem solved or reason for using it. The intent of the State pattern is to allow an object to alter its behavior when its internal state changes. The intent of the Strategy pattern is to encapsulate different algorithms or behaviors and make them interchangeable from the client's perspective. The structure is the same for both solutions.

What distinguishes one pattern from another is the problem solved. You can infer the solution structure and problem solved from the pattern name but you can't infer the pattern name from the solution structure alone.

# Design Pattern Templates

One of the most distinctive features of patterns is the uniform structure used to describe them. For example, the patterns introduced earlier were described using a simple structure with just 4 sections: name, context, problem and solution. Having a consistent format makes it easier to learn, compare and use patterns.

There is no single standard format for documenting design patterns. The format used in this book includes 7 sections:

**Pattern Name** – a short descriptive name. Good names are vital as they form the vocabulary for discussing design.

**Introduction** – the context for the design problem and motivation for learning the pattern.

**Intent** – the design problem addressed by the pattern. This is one of the most important sections as it is the trigger for recognizing when there is an opportunity to use the pattern.

**Solution** – the static structural and dynamic behavioral aspects of the solution. The solution is the essence of the design pattern. Design solutions are typically conveyed using prose and UML class diagrams. UML interaction diagrams are included when collaborations between objects in the pattern are noteworthy.

**Sample Code** – a code fragment showing an example implementation of the pattern. A design is abstract. Sometimes it is easier to understand an abstract concept by inferring the abstraction from a tangible example.

**Discussion** – additional information about the pattern. In order to keep the other sections as concise as possible, secondary material on the pattern is presented in this section. Think of this section as extra for experts.

**Related Patterns** – patterns related to the one being described. Patterns can be related for different reasons. One pattern may fully contain another (Model-View-Controller contains Observer). One pattern may address a problem that is similar to a problem addressed by another pattern (Template Method and Strategy address similar problems). One pattern may have the same structure as another (Strategy has the same structure as State). Knowing the relationships between patterns helps in understanding the subtle distinctions between the patterns.

## Introduction to the Patterns

Ten design patterns are presented here:

1. Singleton
2. Iterator
3. Adapter
4. Decorator
5. State
6. Strategy
7. Factory Method
8. Observer
9. Façade
10. Template Method

I chose these patterns because they are the ones used most often in practice.

# Chapter 2 Singleton

Using the Singleton design pattern to avoid introducing a global variable is like trying to eat healthy at McDonald's by ordering a Big Mac without the bun. Yes, doing so will reduce the calorie count somewhat, but it does little to mitigate the real problem with the meal.

## Introduction

The Singleton design pattern is simple in concept and easy to apply. The typical implementation requires adding just 5-6 statements to an existing class.

The context for the Singleton design pattern is the situation where an application needs a single instance of a given class and a global point of access to it. The classic example is logging.

For the purposes of illustration, assume you have a simple logging class with methods for recording information on different types of events:

```
public class SimpleLog {
    public void info(String message);
    public void error(String message);
}
```

Only one instance of the class is needed and this instance has potential use throughout the program.

One design option is to declare an instance of the class as a global variable and establish conventions for creating and using the global variable.

```
SimpleLog logger;
```

Declaring a global variable would provide convenient access from all points in the program but conventions for access aren't as reliable as language mechanisms that enforce access rules.

A *slightly* better solution is to use the Singleton design pattern. "Slightly" is the operative word here. The Singleton design pattern has some advantages over simply declaring a global variable, but it doesn't completely eliminate all the problems associated with the use of global variables.

When faced with the two criteria for using the Singleton design pattern (single instance and global access) oftentimes the best approach is to first look for ways of restructuring the application such that global access isn't needed. Only after exhausting all reasonable attempts to limit the scope of the class instance, should the Singleton design pattern be used.

The tradeoffs between global variables and singletons are described in more detail in the discussion section below.

## Intent

The Singleton design pattern ensures that not more than one instance of a class is created and provides a global point of access to this instance.

## Solution

To make a class a singleton:

1.  Make the constructor of the class private to prevent clients from creating instances of the class directly.
2.  Add a public static method getInstance() to the class that returns an instance of the class. The first time getInstance() is called an instance of the class is created, cached and returned. On subsequent calls, the cached instance is returned.

Visually, the design of a singleton class looks something like:

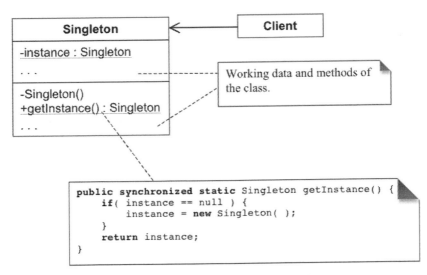

**Figure 19  UML diagram for Singleton design pattern**

In a multithreaded application special care is needed to ensure that getInstance() is thread-safe. The sample implementation shown in

the UML comment box above is thread-safe. The keyword
synchronized on the static method getInstance() means that
when one thread is executing inside the method, all other threads that
attempt to enter getInstance() will block. If the method wasn't
synchronized, it is possible that two threads could check the value of the
class variable instance at the same time, find it null and both attempt to
create an instance of the class Singleton.

One drawback with the implementation above is performance.
Synchronized methods are much slower than non-synchronized ones. In
practice though, unless getInstance() is called repeatedly, the
overhead will be negligible. If performance is an issue, there are three
alternate implementations to consider.

First, if the class doesn't need to support multiple threads of control, the
simplest way of improving performance is to simply take off the key word
synchronized.

```
/* This method is not thread-safe */
public static Singleton getInstance() {
    if( instance == null ) {
        instance = new Singleton( );
    }
    return instance;
}
```

Second, if the overhead of creating the instance of the class is small and/or
the instance will always be created, consider creating the instance at
startup:

```
public class Singleton {
    private static Singleton instance = new Singleton();

    public static Singleton getInstance() {
        return instance;
    }
}
```

The Java runtime guarantees static class variables are initialized before
they are accessible from any thread. One limitation of this solution is that
any data needed to initialize the instance of the singleton must be available
during static initialization.

And finally, the double-checked locking synchronization technique can be
used to speed up the common case. (Those coding in Java should know
that because of a bug in the JVM, double-check locking is not guaranteed
to work in Java 1.4 or earlier.)

```
public class Singleton {
    private volatile static Singleton instance;

    private Singleton {};

    public static Singleton getInstance() {
        if( instance == null ) {
            synchronized {
                if( instance == null ) {
                    instance = new Singleton( );
                }
            }
        }
        return instance;
    }
}
```

Double-checked locking is slightly more complex than using a synchronized method but is more efficient because once the object is create, requests for the object aren't synchronized.

## Sample Code

The following code shows how to implement a simple logging class as a singleton.

```
public class SimpleLog {
    private SimpleLog () {
        // Open log files
        ...
    }

    private static SimpleLog instance = null;

    public synchronized static SimpleLog getInstance() {
        if( instance == null ) {
            instance = new SimpleLog ( );
        }
        return instance;
    }

    // Working methods of the class
    public void synchronized debug(String message ) {
        . . .
    }

    public void synchronized info(String message ) {
        . . .
    }
}
```

**Figure 20  A simple logging class implemented as a singleton**

Clients of the singleton use the static class method getInstance() to access the shared object:

```
public class Client {
    public void f() {
        SimpleLog logService = Simplelog.getInstance();
        logService.debug("Starting Client::f()");
        . . .
    }
}
```

**Figure 21  Sample client code for accessing a singleton**

# Discussion

The Singleton design pattern has the distinction of being not only one of the simplest design patterns, but also ironically one of the most controversial. Much of the controversy stems from a failure to fully appreciate the consequences of using the pattern. The principle problem with the pattern is that it introduces global state into a program. Programmers that don't recognize this may unwittingly use the pattern in situations where there are better design alternatives.

To understand the potential negative consequences associated with improper use of the Singleton design pattern, consider two designs for a class that encapsulates an integer.

Design 1

Design 2

```
public class S {
    int getValue();
    void setValue(int i);
}

S s = new S();
```

```
public class S {
    private static S instance;
    public static S getInstance();
    int getValue();
    void setValue(int i);
}
```

**Figure 22  Comparing use of a global variable to use of a singleton**

The design on the left declares a global variable of type S. The design on the right implements class S as a singleton. Most programmers, even if they don't fully understand all the reasons why, know to avoid global variables whenever possible. So, is the design on the right significantly better than the design on left because it avoids the use of a global variable? The short answer is no. While the design on the right avoids the use of a global variable per se, it still introduces *global state*, and it's the consequences of global state that makes global variables so unpopular.

Using the Singleton design pattern to avoid introducing a global variable is like trying to eat healthy at McDonald's by ordering a Big Mac without the bun. Yes, doing so will reduce the calorie count somewhat, but it does little to mitigate the real problem with the meal.

Figure 23 compares use of a singleton class to the declaration of a global variable in terms of benefits and liabilities. As you can see, a singleton class has more benefits and fewer liabilities than a global variable. However, not all liabilities are created equal (i.e. have equal consequence). The most severe liabilities are those common to both global variables and singleton classes. Consequently, declaring a class as a singleton is only marginally better than declaring a global variable.

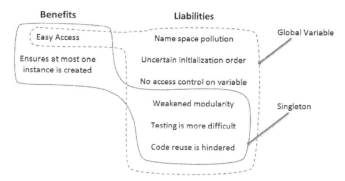

**Figure 23  Benefits and liabilities of singletons and global variables**

One of the main drawbacks with declaring a class as a singleton (and using global variables as well) is that it can introduce hidden dependencies that weaken modularity. Figure 24 shows an example of how shared access to a singleton can create implicit coupling between two modules.

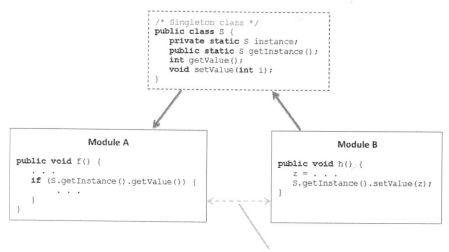

**Figure 24  Implicit coupling caused by shared access to a singleton**

Module A is tightly coupled to module B but you wouldn't know it by looking at just the interfaces of the two modules (or a class diagram of both modules). The coupling is created indirectly through shared access to singleton S.

In a well-modularized system you can study or test one module independent of others. Ideally, in order to study or test module A in the example above, you shouldn't have to look beyond the borders of module A. However, because module A accesses global state in singleton S, you also have to be aware of code in other modules that update this global state. If you want to understand method f() in module A you also have to inspect the code in method h() in module B because h() modifies global state accessed by f(). Notice that the dependency goes beyond the interface to module B. You can't simply study the interface of h() because global state is updated as a side-effect of calling h(). You have to study the detailed implementation of h().

Weakened modularity also complicates testing. In the following code fragment, the class PaymentService is implemented as a singleton. This design makes it hard to test the routine checkout() in isolation. Any tests ran on the routine checkout() are going to affect whatever instance of PaymentService is available. Running a test on checkout() is likely to leave the system in a different state. This can cause havoc with test case ordering, repeatability, debugging, etc.

```java
/* Singleton class */
public class PaymentService {
    private static PaymentService instance;
    public static PaymentService getInstance();
    void invoice(Customer c, float amount);
}

public void checkout(Order o, Customer c) {
    PaymentService ps = PaymentService.getInstance();
    ps.invoice(c, o.getTotal());
}
```

Given the magnitude of the liabilities associated with the Singleton design pattern, you should approach the declaration of a singleton as you would the declaration of a global variable and exhaust all other design alternatives before settling for a singleton. The principle way of avoiding a singleton class is to restructure the code to limit the scope of the object in question. If the object doesn't have to be visible to the whole program, it can be declared local to some class or routine and passed as a parameter to the routines that do need access.

If you do choose to use a singleton in order to avoid passing a frequently used variable from routine to routine, consider making the singleton *semi-global*. Many languages have support for limiting the visibility of a class. For example, in Java declaring a class public makes it visible to the whole program. Declaring a class without an access modifier limits visibility to the package in which it is declared. Remember, the issue isn't that global scope is bad, but rather, that scope should be as narrow as possible. A class variable in a 300-line class is more of a problem than a global variable in a 200-line program.

Something else to consider when balancing the convenience of global access with the advantages of limited scope is how the class will be used. Read-only (immutable) or write-only classes are less of a problem than read/write classes. Classes with read-only data are like global constants. Classes such as loggers that are write-only have no effect on the program's execution. In both cases, what is going on in one section of code has no influence on another section of code. This greatly mitigates the issues with global data.

## Related Patterns

The Singleton design pattern can be used with the Abstract Factory design pattern to guarantee at most one factory class is created. It can also be used with the State design pattern in order to avoid recreating state classes when the state switches.

# Chapter 3  Iterator

## Introduction

The iterator design pattern provides a way of traversing the elements of a collection object without exposing the underlying implementation.

A collection object (also called a container object) is an object that stores a group of related items. There are standard types of collection objects such as lists, sets and dictionaries as well as user-defined collection objects that group application-specific elements. For example, an application might have a `ProductPortfolio` class that groups related products:

```
public class ProductPortfolio {
   private Product products[];
   . . .
}
```

Clients of collection objects often need to visit each element of the collection. One way for a collection class like `ProductPortfolio` to support traversal of its elements is to simply give clients access to its internal data structure.

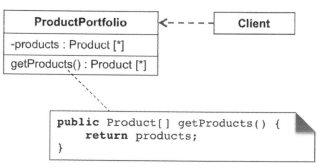

**Figure 25  First candidate design for traversing the elements of a collection class**

The following code fragment shows the implementation of the collection along with client code that traverses the elements of the collection:

```
public class ProductPortfolio {
   private Product products[];
   // Not recommended. Promotes high coupling
   public Product[] getProducts() {
      return products;
   }
}
```

```
void static clientCode(ProductPortfolio portfolio) {
    Product products[] = portfolio.getProducts();
    for (int i=0; i<products.size; i++)
        process(products[i]);
}
```

The main problem with this solution is it violates the principle of information hiding. Giving clients access to the internal data structure used to store product data increases coupling between clients and ProductPortfolio. This causes two potential problems. First, there is no language mechanism preventing clients from directly adding or deleting products from the internal data structure. Second, the cost of making changes to the internal data structure of ProductPortfolio goes up with each new client access. Should the internal implementation change from an array to say a linked list, all clients accessing the original array will also have to be updated to work with a linked list rather than an array. (Alternately, ProductPortfolio could create and return an array from the internal linked list, but this would be less efficient.)

## Intent

The Iterator design pattern solves the problem of how to traverse the elements of a collection object in a way that keeps client code doing the traversing loosely coupled to the collection object as well as the traversal algorithm.

## Solution

Rather than present the general design for the Iterator design pattern straightaway, it will be evolved from the example presented in the introduction. Doing so will provide some justification for why the final design looks the way it does as well as serve as a simple example of how design principles can be used to guide the design process.

As mentioned in the introduction, one way of supporting iteration is to simply give clients access to the internal data structure of the collection class. This design option is unappealing because it increases coupling between clients and the collection. One way of addressing this problem is to keep the internal data structure private and add traversal methods to the interface of the collection.

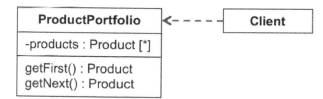

**Figure 26 Second candidate design for traversing the elements of a collection class**

Clients would use the traversal methods of the collection to visit each element of the collection:

```
public class ProductPortfolio {
    private Product products[];
    . . .

    // Return first product or null
    public Product getFirst() { . . . }

    // Return next product or null
    public Product getNext() { . . . }
}

void static clientCode(ProductPortfolio portfolio) {
    Product product = portfolio.getFirst();

    while (product != null) {
        process(product);
        product = portfolio.getNext();
    }
}
```

While this solution better insolates clients from the implementation details of ProductPortfolio, it violates another principle of good design, which is the single responsibility principle. Including iteration logic in ProductPortfolio makes it responsible not only for operations specific to product portfolios (not shown) but also iteration.

To remedy this problem, iteration logic can be extracted from ProductPortfolio and placed in a separate class, Iterator.

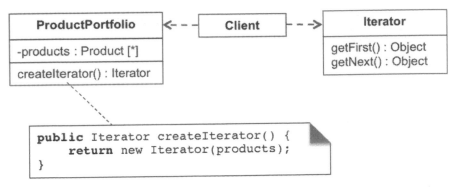

**Figure 27  Third candidate design for traversing the elements of a collection class**

The traversal algorithm now resides in the class Iterator. To traverse the elements of ProductPortfolio, clients call the factory method createIterator() to request an iterator object and use the iterator object to traverse the elements in the container.

```
public class ProductPortfolio {
    private Product products[];
    . . .

    public Iterator createIterator() {
        return new Iterator(products)
    }
}

public class Iterator {
    private Product products[];
    . . .

    public Iterator(Product products[]) {
        this.products = products;
    }

    // Return first product or null
    public Product getFirst() { . . . }

    // Return next product or null
    public Product getNext() { . . . }
}
```

```
void clientCode(ProductPortfolio portfolio) {
    Iterator iterator = portfolio.createIterator();
    Product product = iterator.getFirst();

    while (product != null) {
        process(product);
        product = iterator.getNext();
    }
}
```

This design has a couple of other benefits besides having a cohesive container class. Representing iteration logic in a separate class makes it possible to have multiple iterations in progress on the same container. It also makes it possible for containers with similar implementation to reuse or share the same iterator.

While the current design doesn't violate any major design principles, it is somewhat inflexible. Oftentimes there are multiple types of collection classes and multiple types of iteration algorithms. As it is now, client code is tightly coupled to a specific type of container (ProductPortfolio) and a specific type of iteration (Iterator). Clients that just need to traverse the elements of a collection and don't care about the specific type of collection or iteration algorithm would benefit from more generality in the design.

The design can be made more flexible by adding abstract interfaces for container types and iteration algorithms.

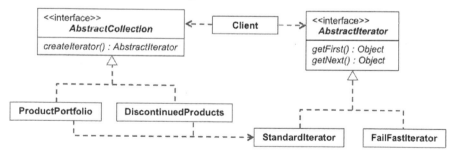

**Figure 28  Application-specific example of Iterator design pattern**

Client code written in terms of the abstract interfaces AbstractCollection and AbstractItertor will work with any specific type of collection or iteration that conforms to these abstractions.

The following code fragment demonstrates polymorphic client code that works with instances of ProductPortfolio,

DiscontinuedProducts and instances of any other class that implements the interface AbstractCollection.

```
interface AbstractCollection {
    AbstractIterator createIterator();
}

interface AbstractIterator {
    Product getFirst();
    Product getNext();
}

class ProductPortfolio implements AbstractCollection {
    private Product products[];
    public AbstractIterator createIterator() {
        return new StandardIterator(products);
    }
}

class DiscontinuedProducts implements
AbstractCollection {
    private Product products[];
    public AbstractIterator createIterator() {
        return new StandardIterator(products);
    }
}

class StandardIterator implements AbstractIterator {
    . . .
    public StandardIterator(Product products[]) {
        . . .
    }
    public Object getFirst() {
        . . .
    }
    public Object getNext() {
        . . .
    }
}
```

```
// Polymorphic client code.
// This method works for any object that
//    implements the interface AbstractCollection.
public static void clientCode(AbstractCollection c) {

    AbstractIterator iterator = c.createIterator();
    Object item = iterator.getFirst();

    while (item != null) {
        process(item);
        item = iterator.getNext();
    }
}

public static void main(String[] args) {
    DiscontinuedProducts dp = new
    DiscontinuedProducts();
    ProductPortfolio pp = new ProductPortfolio();
    . . .
    clientCode(dp);
    clientCode(pp);
}
```

The code fragment above also demonstrates flexibility with respect to the iteration algorithm used. Both ProductPortfolio and DiscountinuedProducts return an instance of StandardIteration, but since the client routine is written in terms of AbstractIterator, it will work with any iteration algorithm that implements the interface AbstractIterator.

The UML diagram in Figure 28 shows a box for FailFastIterator. Fail fast iteration is a safer form of iteration that throws an exception if the container is updated during iteration. ProductPortfolio could be modified to return an instance of FailFastIterator and the client code would work just fine.

The previous example introduced the iterator design pattern with an application-specific example. The structure diagram for the more general Iterator design pattern is shown in Figure 29.

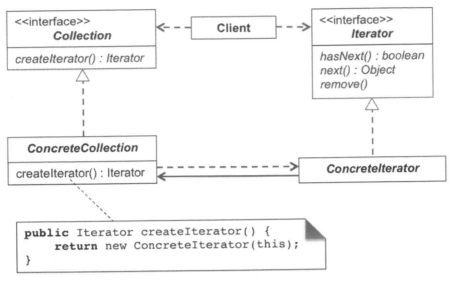

**Figure 29  Structure diagram for the Iterator design pattern**

The Iterator design pattern has four components:

**Collection** – defines the interface for collection types. Included in the interface is createIterator(), a factory method for creating the iterator for the collection. Optionally, the interface may also include methods for managing (adding, removing, etc.) the elements of the collection.

**Iterator** –defines the interface for traversing the elements of a collection. There is no standard set of methods for iteration. The iterator interface in the Java API (Iterator) consists of hasNext(), next() and remove(). The iterator interface in the .NET framework (IEnumerator) consists of the attribute Current and the methods MoveNext() and Reset(). Some iterators also allow forward and backward traversal.

**ConcreteCollection** – a class that implements the Collection interface. The concrete collection decides which iterator to create.

**ConcreteIterator** – a class that implements the Iterator interface. A concrete iterator needs access to the internal data structure of the collection it traverses. A collection may grant its iterator privileged access to its internals (e.g. by friending the iterator in C++ or defining a nested class in Java) or pass a reference or copy of its internal data structure as an argument to the iterator's constructor. How's this different from giving clients access to the internal details of iterators? Granting an iterator privileged access is less of a concern because in general there will be many more clients than iterators.

## Sample Code

Most object-oriented programming languages include support for collections. Those that do typically offer an assortment of concrete collection classes (e.g. Array, LinkedList, and Dictionary) along with abstractions (e.g. interfaces) for collections and their iterators. Figure 30 shows some of the key classes and interfaces in the Java collection framework.

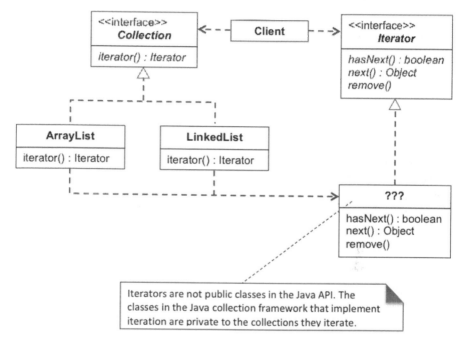

**Figure 30  Key classes and interfaces in the Java collection framework**

The following Java program demonstrates polymorphic client code traversing the elements of two completely different data structures.

```java
// Output:
// 1 2
// 3 4
import java.util.*;

public class IteratorExample
{
    public static void main(String[] args)
    {
        ArrayList arrayList = new ArrayList();
        arrayList.add(new Integer(1));
        arrayList.add(new Integer(2));

        LinkedList linkedList = new LinkedList();
        linkedList.add(new Integer(3));
        linkedList.add(new Integer(4));

        clientCode(arrayList);
        clientCode(linkedList);
    }

    public static void clientCode(Collection collection)
    {
        Iterator i = collection.iterator();
        while (i.hasNext())
        {
            Object o = i.next();
            String s = o.toString();
            System.out.print(s + " ");
        }
        System.out.println();
    }
}
```

## Discussion

The Iterator design pattern illustrates just how far some design patterns have come. The iterator design pattern, like all patterns, started out as a general solution to a reoccurring design problem. Later, support for the pattern began to appear in language class libraries. Today, several programming languages include support for the pattern in the language proper.

For example, C# includes a foreach statement, which is used to iterate over the elements of a collection or array:

```
foreach (ItemType item in someCollection)
```

someCollection is any object that implements the interface
IEnumerable or declares the method GetEnumerator(). The
interface IEnumberable has one method that returns an iterator of type
IEnumerator:

```
interface IEnumerable {
    IEnumerator GetEnumerator();
}

interface IEnumcrator {
    Object Current {get;}
    bool MoveNext();
    void Reset();
}
```

Here is a complete example showing the application-specific collection
ProductPortfolio being used with the foreach statement. Notice
that ProductPortfolio creates and returns an iterator.

```
// Output:
// Pencil   $0.5
// Eraser   $1
// Notebook  $2
using System;
using System.Collections;
class Program {
    static void Main(string[] args) {
        ProductPortfolio currentProducts = new
            ProductPortfolio();
        foreach (Product p in currentProducts)
            Console.WriteLine(p.name + "   $" + p.amount);
        Console.ReadLine();
    }
}

public class Product {
    public string name;
    public double amount;
    public Product(string name, double amount) {
        this.name = name;
        this.amount = amount;
    }
}

public class ProductPortfolio : IEnumerable {
    private Product[] products;
```

```
public ProductPortfolio() {
    products = new Product[3] {
        new Product("Pencil",.5),
        new Product("Eraser",1.0),
        new Product("Notebook",2.0) };
}

public IEnumerator GetEnumerator() {
    return new StandardIterator(products);
}

private class StandardIterator : IEnumerator {
    private Product[] products;
    private int position;

    public StandardIterator(Product[] products) {
        this.products = products;
        Reset();
    }

    public bool MoveNext() {
        position++;
        return (position < products.Length);
    }

    public void Reset() { position = -1; }

    public object Current {
        get { return products[position]; }
    }
}
}
```

## Related Patterns

The createIterator() method of the Collection interface is a factory
method. Concrete collection classes decide which concrete iterator to
create and return.

# Chapter 4  Adapter

## Introduction

Before MP3s, before compact disks, before cassette tapes, the standard format for portable audio was the 8-track tape.

**Figure 31  Eight-track tape cartridge**

Eight-track tapes were popular in the United States from the mid 60's to the late 1970's. During the late 1970's, smaller more versatile cassette tapes gradually replaced 8-track tapes as the format of choice for portable audio.

During the transition from 8-track tapes to cassette tapes, music consumers faced some tough choices. When should they start buying cassette tapes rather than 8-track tapes? When should they purchase a cassette player? It cost more to be an early adopter, but waiting longer means having more music in the soon-to-be-obsolete format.

Manufactures offered at least a partial solution in the form of an 8-track tape player adapter. The adapter made it possible to play a cassette tape in an 8-track tape player. One end of the adapter plugged into the 8-track tape player and in the middle was a slot for inserting a cassette tape.

**Figure 32  Eight-track to cassette adapter**

The adapter converted an 8-track interface into a cassette interface. It converted the interface available into the interface needed:

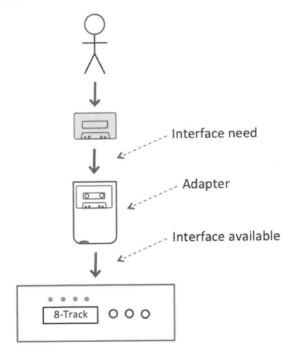

Interface need

Adapter

Interface available

8-Track

**Figure 33  An adapter converts an interface that is available into an interface that is needed**

Eight-track tape player adapters smoothed the transition from 8-track tapes to cassettes. Users didn't have to upgrade their stereo equipment and media at the same time. Adapters allowed them to prolong the life of their 8-track tape players and start purchasing cassettes sooner than they otherwise might have.

The adapter design pattern can do the same for your software investments. A software system consists of numerous modules connected via interfaces. Sometimes a needed service is available but offered through an interface that is incompatible with existing code. When there is a mismatch between the interface available and the interface needed, the adapter design pattern can be used to make the interface available look and act like the interface needed.

Here is an example to illustrate the point.

Imagine you want to write a Java program that displays the contents of your computer's file system. Because file system data is hierarchical, the most suitable Swing user interface control for this task is the JTree control.

**Figure 34  JTree view of a file system**

A JTree object is only responsible for the view. The data displayed resides in a separate object, a data model that conforms to the TreeModel interface.

**View**                          **Model**

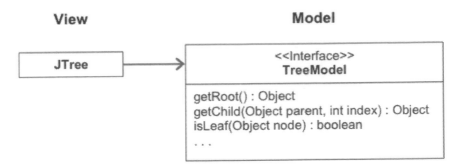

**Figure 35  The data model for the JTree view is of type TreeModel**

The file system data to be displayed by the proposed Java program resides in a tree of File objects.

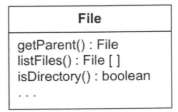

**Figure 36  File system data resides in objects of type File**

An instance of File represents a file or directory in the file system tree. From any one file or directory it is possible to navigate to any other file or directory in the file system. The methods defined for file are similar to those in the interface TreeModel, but unfortunately File doesn't implement the interface TreeModel. If it did, we could use it directly with JTree. All the data needed to display a tree view of the file system is available from an instance of File, it's just not available through the needed interface.

This is the perfect opportunity to use the Adapter design pattern. Applying the Adapter pattern here results in an adapter class that converts File's interface into the TreeModel interface.

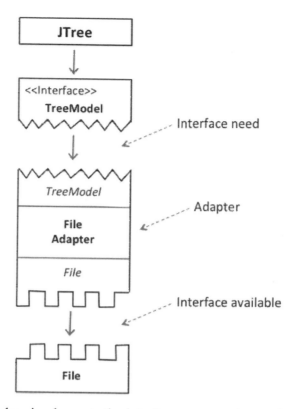

The adapter class implements the interface TreeModel and wraps an instance of File. Since it implements TreeModel it can serve as the data model for an instance of JTree. Requests made of the adapter class are delegated to the wrapped instance of File.

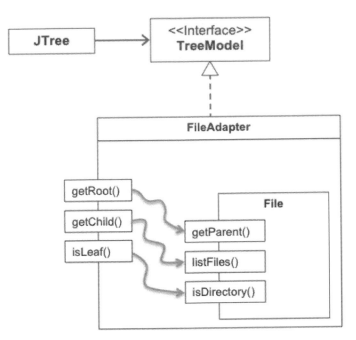

**Figure 37  Conceptual class diagram for Adapter design pattern**

# Intent

The Adapter design pattern is useful in situations where an existing class provides a needed service but there is a mismatch between the interface offered and the interface clients expect. The Adapter pattern shows how to convert the interface of the existing class into the interface clients expect.

# Solution

There are two different ways of implementing the Adapter design pattern, one using composition and the other using inheritance.

With composition, the adapter class implements the interface clients expect. At runtime the adapter object is initialized with a reference to the service available. Clients call operations on the adapter object and the adapter object forwards these calls to the service available.

Visually, adaptation via composition looks something like:

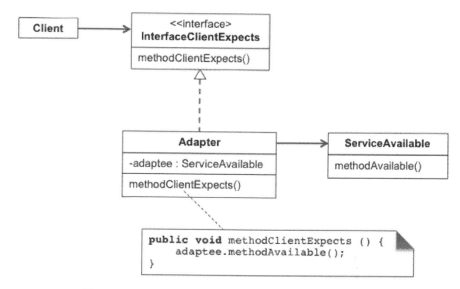

**Figure 38  Adapter pattern using object composition**

Figure 39 shows the class diagram for an 8-track to cassette adapter implemented using object composition. Notice that one operation— reverse() —is handled in the adapter class rather than the adapted class. Eight-track tape players don't have a reverse function. Even though the spirit of the Adapter pattern is to simply pass operations on to the adaptee, the adapter may take responsibility for some or all of an operation.

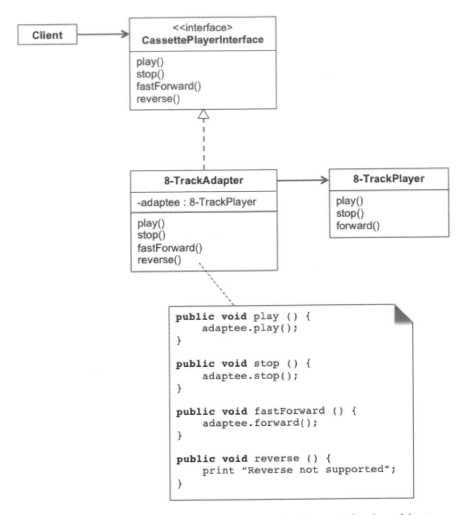

**Figure 39  Eight-track to cassette adapter implemented using object composition**

With inheritance, the adapter class implements the interface the client expects (or inherits the interface from an existing class if the programming language being used allows multiple inheritance) and inherits from the class representing the service available. Clients call operations on the adapter object and the adapter object forwards these calls as necessary to the inherited operations of the available service.

Visually, adaptation via inheritance looks something like:

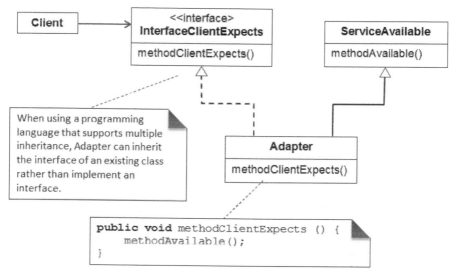

**Figure 40  Adapter pattern using class inheritance**

Figure 41 shows the class diagram for an 8-track to cassette adapter implemented using class inheritance. Notice that delegate code isn't needed in the adapter class for operations on the client interface that are identical to operations in the inherited service.

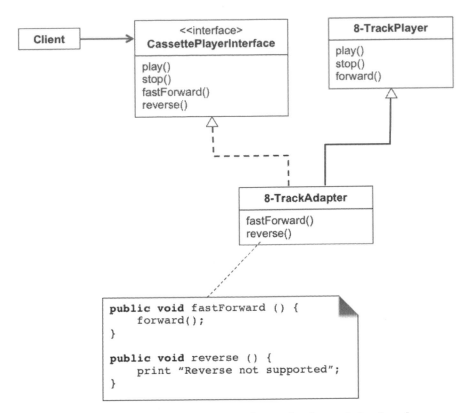

**Figure 41  Eight-track to cassette adapter implemented using class inheritance**

Implementing the adapter pattern with inheritance rather than composition requires less code when methods in the expected interface are already implemented in the adaptee. However, because inheritance exposes the protected interface of a parent class to subclasses, inheritance also creates the potential for tighter coupling between the adapter and the adaptee. For example, suppose 8-TrackPlayer had a protected field for the position of the playback head:

| 8-TrackPlayer |
| --- |
| # timePosition : int |
| play()<br>stop()<br>forward() |

The adapter class is free to make use of this protected information when implementing its own methods:

```
public void fastForward() {
   timePosition = timePosition + 5;
}
```

The result is tighter coupling between the adapter and the adaptee. Because higher coupling is typically more harmful than a few extra lines of simple delegate code, composition is usually a better option than inheritance when implementing the adapter design pattern.

In general, when the only purpose of using inheritance is reuse, composition is usually a more appropriate implementation strategy. Situations like this are why some experts encourage designers to: *favor object composition over class inheritance* (Gamma, et al. 1995), or as I like to say, *always consider object composition before resorting to class inheritance.*

## Sample Code

The sample code in this section implements the file system display example mentioned in the introduction.

Recall that the standard Java user interface component for displaying hierarchical data is JTree. Also recall that JTree is just the view. The data displayed is stored in a separate object that implements the TreeModel interface. The Adapter pattern is needed because File, the class with the file system data, doesn't implement the TreeModel interface.

In the code below, FileAdapter implements the TreeModel interface and wraps an instance of File. Requests for data from JTree are forwarded to the wrapped instance of File. Note, not all of the methods in the interface TreeModel are implemented by the adapter. Specifically, methods needed to handle dynamic changes to the underlying data model are not implemented. Also note the extra code needed in the delegate methods to make the existing interface function like the expected interface. Delegation isn't always as simple as calling an identical method of a different name.

```
import java.awt.*;
import javax.swing.event.*;
import java.io.*;
import javax.swing.*;
import javax.swing.tree.*;
```

```java
public class FileAdapterExample extends JFrame {
   public static void main(String[] args) {
      new FileAdapterExample();
   }

   public FileAdapterExample() {
      JTree tree;
      FileAdapter treeNode;

      Container content = getContentPane();

      // start at the root of the file system
      File f = new File("/");
      treeNode = new FileAdapter (f);
      tree = new JTree(treeNode);

      content.add(new
      JScrollPane(tree),BorderLayout.CENTER);
      setSize(600, 375);
      setVisible(true);
   }
}

class FileAdapter implements TreeModel {
   // root of displayed tree
   private File root;

   public FileAdapter (File file) {
      root = file;
   }

   public Object getRoot() {
      return root;
   }

   public Object getChild(Object parent, int index) {
      File files[] = ((File)parent).listFiles();
      return files[index];
   }

   public int getChildCount(Object parent) {
      File files[] = ((File)parent).listFiles();
      if (files == null)
         return 0;
      else
         return files.length;
   }
```

```
public boolean isLeaf(Object node) {
    return !((File)node).isDirectory();
}

public void valueForPathChanged(TreePath path,
Object newValue) { }

public int getIndexOfChild(Object parent, Object
child) {
    return 0;
}

public void addTreeModelListener(TreeModelListener
l) { }

public void
removeTreeModelListener(TreeModelListener l) { }
}
```

## Discussion

The Adapter design pattern provides a convenient solution to the problem of how to upgrade interdependent system components at different rates. For example, suppose you have a program with two classes A and B as shown in the following image. Class A is dependent on class B because a method in class A calls a method in class B. Furthermore, suppose you plan to rename the method g() in B to h(). This will necessitate changes to both A and B:

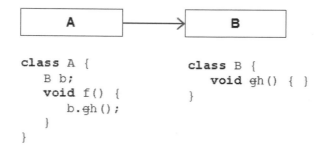

```
class A {              class B {
    B b;                   void g̶h() { }
    void f() {         }
        b.g̶h();
    }
}
```

Any change to software introduces some risk, and the more components or classes that change at one time, the greater the risk. One way to reduce this risk is to integrate and test the changes one component at a time.

Let's say you decide to integrate and test changes to B before making changes to A. This can be accomplished by making the changes to B and then adding an adapter to make the new interface of B look like the old one.

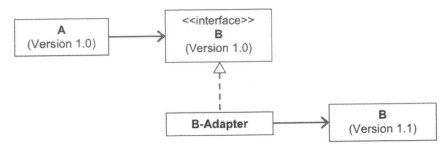

The changes to B can be integrated and fully tested before integrating the updates to A. When you are ready to integrate changes to A, simply remove the adapter and allow the new version of A to interact directly with the updated version of B.

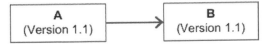

## Related Patterns

The Adapter, Bridge, Proxy and Facade patterns have the same basic structure and collaboration. Requests to a subject object are forwarded on to a delegate object.

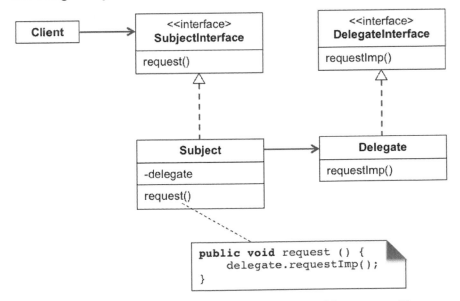

**Figure 42  Several design patterns are based on object composition**

While the structure and interaction diagrams for these four patterns may look similar, the patterns are distinguished by their intent or purpose.

The intent of the Adapter pattern is to resolve incompatibilities between two existing interfaces. With the Adapter pattern Client and Delegate are two existing classes that needed to work together but can't because of incompatible interfaces. The Adapter pattern converts the interface of Delegate into the existing SubjectInterface so that Delegate objects can be used (or reused) with clients expecting objects that implement SubjectInterface.

The intent of the Bridge pattern is to separate an interface from its implementation so the two can vary independently. With the Bridge pattern, in contrast with the Adapter pattern, the interfaces SubjectInterface and DelegateInterface don't exist at the time the pattern is applied. The design of these two interfaces is the whole point of the Bridge pattern. The result of using the Bridge pattern is the ability for the abstraction defined by SubjectInterface and implementation defined in Delegate to evolve independently.

The intent of the Proxy pattern is to provide a surrogate or placeholder for another object in order to control access to it. With the Proxy pattern, SubjectInterface and DelegateInterface are one and the same. Classes Subject and Delegate implement the same interface. Subject controls access to Delegate and is therefore considered a proxy for Delegate.

The intent of the Facade pattern is to provide a simplified interface to one or more classes. With the Facade pattern, SubjectInterface is the new simplified interface that is created in order to simplify access to Delegate classes. Façade doesn't hide or encapsulate Delegate. Delegate is still accessible through the more complex DelegateInterface.

Another pattern that shares some similarities with the Adapter pattern is Decorator. Both Decorator and Adapter wrap another object, but they do so for different reasons. Adapter wraps an object to change its interface. Decorator wraps an object to add behavior.

# Chapter 5 Decorator

## Introduction

The Decorator design pattern uses object composition and delegation to extend the behavior of existing classes in a way that is both lightweight and flexible. To understand the value of this approach, consider the other options for extending the behavior of a class.

The most straightforward way of extending the behavior of a class is to simply modify the class to include the new behavior. For example, the class in Figure 43 offers features A, B and C. Adding a new feature is a simple matter of adding the code for the new feature. The biggest problem with this approach is that it violates the open-closed principle. The open-closed principle states that classes should be open for extension, but closed for modification. Because adding a new feature requires changing the exiting class, the class clearly is not closed for modification. Designs that follow the open closed principle are preferred because there is less risk of collateral damage when adding new features.

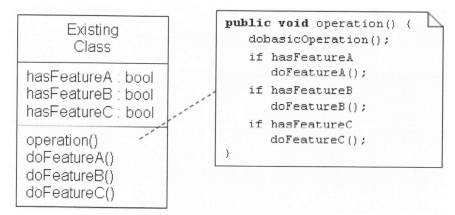

**Figure 43 Adding new features requires changing existing code**

Another option for extending the behavior of an existing class is inheritance. With inheritance, class behavior is extended by adding a subclass and overriding one or more methods in the base class.

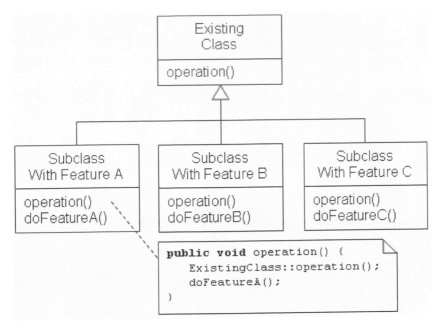

**Figure 44  Adding new features via subclassing**

Adding new features via subclassing complies with the open-closed principle because behavior is extended without making changes to existing code. However, because the protected interface of the base class is exposed to subclasses, inheritance tends to weaken the encapsulation barrier around the base class—a condition known as the fragile superclass problem. When extending behavior via inheritance, existing classes are more vulnerable to change than with other methods such as delegation where dependencies are limited only to the public interface of classes.

Another disadvantage of using inheritance to extend the behavior of a class is that it creates a compile-time structural relationship between the features being added and the classes being extended. Feature combinations must be anticipated at design time. That is more rigid than adding and removing features at runtime via object composition.

One final situation where inheritance performs poorly is when different combinations of features are valid. The main problem is the potential for a combinatorial explosion of subclasses. For example, Figure 45 shows 7 different subclasses--one for each combination of features A, B and C.

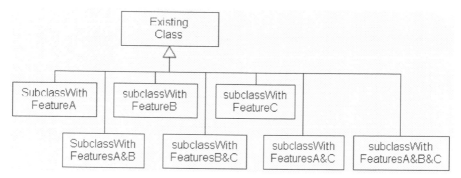

**Figure 45  Inheritance doesn't work well when different combinations of features are valid**

The examples above highlight some of the weaknesses associated with common approaches to extending the behavior of a class. The Decorator design pattern provides an alternate approach that addresses many of these weaknesses.

To better understand the concept behind the Decorator design pattern, consider the following fictional account of how an online retailor used the Decorator design pattern to simplify product development.

Once upon a time there was an online retailer planning to offer e-book readers in 3 basic form factors:

1. Standard E-book
2. Large E-book
3. Tablet

This retailer also planned to offer various feature combinations with each base model:

1. Wi-Fi
2. 3G Wireless
3. Discrete text advertisements for $30 off

With 3 base models and 3 optional features, there were 24 (3 * 2^3) different configurations that needed to be manufactured: Standard, Standard + Wi-Fi, Standard + Wi-Fi + 3G, Standard + 3G, etc. Some might be less popular than others, but since the retailer was going after the long tail, it was important to offer all configurations.

Trying to solve the problem using inheritance would result in a very unwieldy inheritance hierarchy:

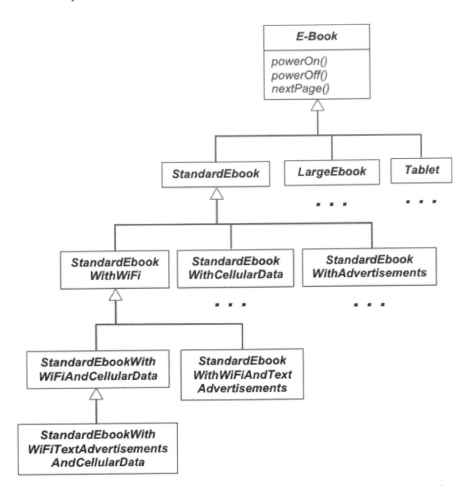

**Figure 46  Trying to accommodate different feature combinations results in an unwieldy inheritance hierarchy**

Not looking forward to the prospect of designing and maintaining 24 different individual device configurations, our fictional retailer challenged its engineers to come up with a breakthrough design that would not only make it easy to configure the current 24 different retail options but also reduce the effort needed to add new features and base models in the future.

The engineers did not disappoint. They proposed a brilliant design with 3 separate base units (standard, large and tablet) and "skins" for each feature. A skin is an invisible slipcover that adds a particular feature. When a customer orders say a Standard E-book with Wi-Fi and discrete text advertisements, a warehouse worker would take a Standard base E-book from a bin and add two transparent slipcovers, one for Wi-Fi and another for discrete text advertisements. Because the slipcovers are transparent and offer the same basic interface as the base unit, customers are unaware that certain features are being added with slipcovers.

Congratulations! You now understand the basic concept behind the decorator design pattern. The decorator design pattern provides a way of attaching additional responsibilities to an object dynamically. Objects to be extended are wrapped with decorator objects. A decorator object implements the same interface as the object it decorates. New features are added before, after or in place of delegating requests to the wrapped object. Figure 47 shows a conceptual diagram for a standard E-book reader decorated with discreet advertisements and Wi-Fi.

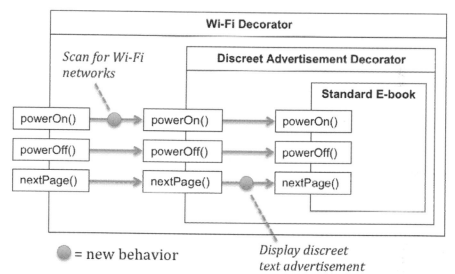

**Figure 47  Conceptual diagram for Decorator design pattern**

## Intent

The Decorator design pattern provides an alternative to class inheritance for extending the behavior of existing classes. It uses object composition rather than class inheritance for a lightweight flexible approach to adding responsibilities to objects at runtime. It is especially useful when different combinations and permutations of features are permitted.

## Solution

Figure 48 shows the main components and general structure of the Decorator design pattern.

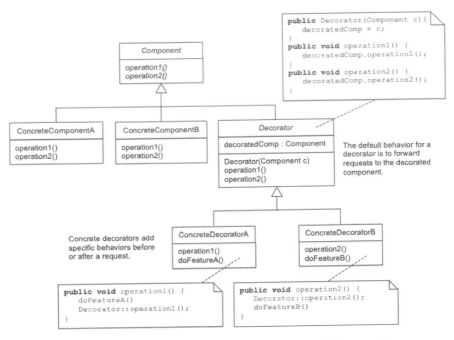

**Figure 48  General structure of the Decorator design pattern**

The two main groups of classes in the Decorator design pattern are concrete components and concrete decorators. Concrete components contain the base functionality that is extended or decorated with features defined in concrete decorators.

To add a feature to a component, you create an instance of the component and pass this instance to the constructor for the decorator that defines the feature you want to add to the component.

```
ConcreteComponent cc = new ConcretComponent();
ConcreteDecorator decoratedComponent = new
ConcreteDecorator(cc);
```

Concrete decorators inherit from the abstract class `Decorator`. `Decorator` is a convenience class. It keeps a reference to the component being decorated and implements the same interface as the component. This allows decorator objects to be used transparently anywhere component objects are expected.

The default behavior for a decorator is to forward requests to the decorated component. Concrete decorators inherit the default decorator behavior and optionally add their own behavior before, after or in place of this default behavior.

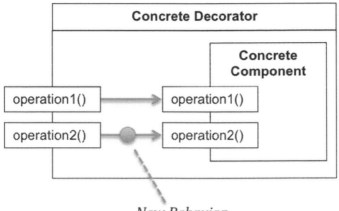

*New Behavior*

Decorators wrap components, which may be concrete components or other decorators. This makes it possible to have an arbitrarily long chain of decorators leading to a concrete component at the end.

The UML sequence diagram in Figure 49 shows the interactions of a concrete component and two decorators. ConcreteDecorator1 adds feature A and ConcreteDecorator2 adds feature B. Not shown in the sequence diagram is the setup logic that configured the concrete component with two decorators:

```
ConcreteComponent cc = new ConcretComponent();
ConcreteDecorator1 cd1 = new ConcreteDecorator2(cc);
ConcreteDecorator2 cd2 = new ConcreteDecorator1(cd1);
cd2.operation();
```

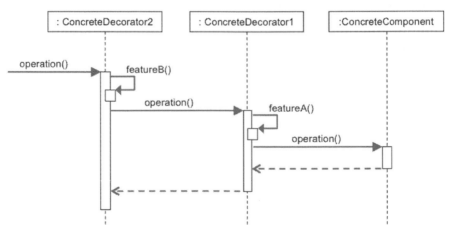

**Figure 49  Behavior diagram for the Decorator design pattern**

## Sample Code

The introduction made the case for using the Decorator design pattern rather than inheritance to achieve a more flexible design for an imaginary line of E-book readers. Figure 50 shows the class diagram for the design. Notice it has three concrete components (StandardEbook, LargeEbook and Tablet) and three concrete decorators (Wi-Fi, 3GWireless and DiscreetAdvertisements).

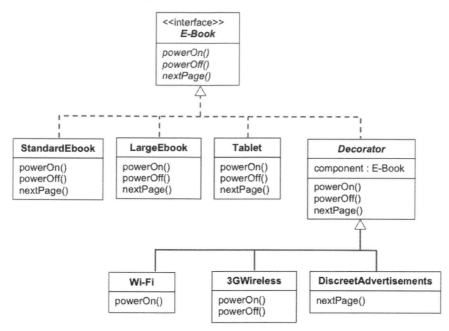

**Figure 50  Class diagram for line of E-book readers using Decorator design pattern**

The following program implements the design and demonstrates its use by decorating a Standard E-book with Wi-Fi and discreet text advertisements. The decorated component searches for Wi-Fi networks when powered on and displays a discreet text advertisement when transitioning from one page to the next. Figure 47 in the introduction shows a conceptual diagram for the implementation below.

```java
public class DecoratorExample {

    public static void main(String[] args) {
        StandardEbook baseModel = new StandardEbook();
        E_Book decoratedEbook = new Wi_Fi(
        new DiscreetAdvertisements (baseModel));
        decoratedEbook.powerOn();
        decoratedEbook.nextPage();
        decoratedEbook.powerOff();
    }
}

interface E_Book {
    void powerOn();
    void powerOff();
    void nextPage();
}

abstract class Decorator implements E_Book {
    private E_Book component;

    public Decorator (E_Book ebook) {
        component = ebook;
    }

    public void powerOn() {
        component.powerOn();
    }

    public void powerOff() {
        component.powerOff();
    }

    public void nextPage() {
        component.nextPage();
    }
}
```

```java
// Concrete Component
class StandardEbook implements E_Book {
    public void powerOn() {
        System.out.println("Power on Standard E-Book");
    }
    public void powerOff() {
        System.out.println("Power off Standard E-Book");
    }
    public void nextPage() {
        System.out.println("Next page Standard E-Book");
    }
}

// Concrete Decorator
class Wi_Fi extends Decorator {
    public Wi_Fi(E_Book component) {
        super (component);
    }
    public void powerOn() {
        super.powerOn();
        System.out.println("Scan for Wi-Fi networks");
    }
}

// Concrete Decorator
class DiscreetAdvertisements extends Decorator {
    public DiscreetAdvertisements(E_Book component) {
        super (component);
    }

    public void nextPage() {
        super.nextPage();
        System.out.println("Advertisement: Buy more stuff
        today!");
    }
}
```

## Discussion

One of the benefits of knowing certain design patterns is that it makes it easier to learn class libraries based on these patterns. The Decorator design pattern illustrates this well. Developers not familiar with the Decorator design pattern are often overwhelmed by the vast number of classes that make up the Java I/O class library. Those familiar with the Decorator design pattern have a much easier time of learning how to use Java I/O classes because the library is based on the Decorator design pattern.

Figure 51 shows some of the key byte stream input data classes in the java.io package. Seeing the classes organized according to the structure of the Decorator design pattern makes it easier to understand the function of each one.

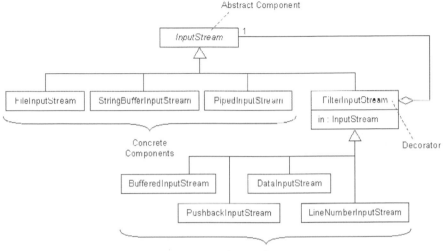

**Figure 51  Classes in the java.io package follow the Decorator design pattern**

The concrete components in Figure 51 represent input sources of raw data. The concrete decorators represent features that can be added to input streams. The concrete components can be decorated with different combinations and permutations of features offered by the concrete decorators. For example, the code fragment below shows a file input stream wrapped with features for buffering and pushing back or "unreading" data.

```
FileInputStream f = new FileInputStream("input.txt");
BufferedInputStream b = new BufferedInputStream(f);
PushbackInputStream p = new PushbackInputStream(b);

int c = p.read();
while (c != ' ') {
    // Process c
    . . .
    c = p.read();
}
// Push back non-blank character read.
p.unread(c);
```

This example also brings to light one of the downsides of using the Decorator design pattern: users must contend with a large number of small classes even for routine tasks. In the example above, three classes had to be constructed and linked just to read bytes from a file.

## Related Patterns

Both Decorator and Adapter delegate requests to a wrapped object. The principle difference between the two patterns is Decorator adds new behavior without changing the interface whereas Adapter keeps the same basic behavior but changes the interface.

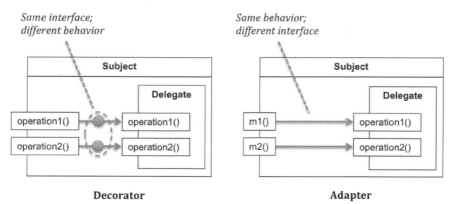

**Figure 52  Principle difference between Decorator and Adapter**

The Factory method design pattern is sometimes used with the Decorator design pattern in order to encapsulate the setup procedure needed to construct and link decorated components. For example, here is a Factory method for constructing a decorated E-book:

```
public E_Book getFeaturedModel() {
    return new Wi_Fi(
        new DiscreetAdvertisements (
        new StandardEbook()));
}
```

# Chapter 6  State

## Introduction

If you want to turn heads at the lake, drive up and then in with an Amphicar.

**Figure 53  Amphicar entering a lake (Photo Credit: Chris McEvoy)**

Sometimes described as the fastest car on the water and the fastest boat on the road, the Amphicar is the world's only civilian mass-produced amphibious automobile.

The mechanics are simple. Torque from the engine is routed through a special land/water transmission to the rear wheels or twin propellers mounted just under the rear bumper. The front tires steer the car on land as well as in the water.

How would you model such a conveyance?

You could lump all the behavior in one class Amphicar. Or, if your programming language supports multiple inheritance, you could store boat behavior in one class and car behavior in another and inherit from both:

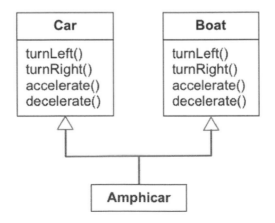

However, neither of these solutions captures the true nature of the vehicle. An Amphicar is both a car and a boat, but it's not both at the same time. On land it acts like a car and in the water it acts like boat. During normal use it may switch back and forth several times between being a car and being a boat. A better way of modeling the behavior of this vehicle is with the State design pattern.

## Intent

Objects have state and behavior. Objects change their state based on internal and external events. If an object goes through clearly identifiable states, and the object's behavior is especially dependent on its state, it is a good candidate for the State design pattern.

## Solution

The solution is to encapsulate state-specific behavior into separate objects and have the context (the object that goes through identifiable states) delegate state-specific requests to these objects.

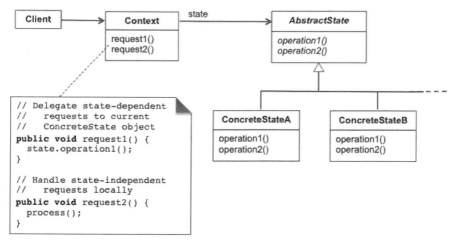

**Figure 54  Structure diagram for State design pattern**

A separate concrete state class is created for each identifiable state of the context. State-specific behavior is encapsulated in these classes. The context defines the interface of interest to clients. It keeps a reference to the state object for the current state of the context. State-dependent requests from clients are forwarded to the current state object. State-independent requests from clients are handled locally in the context. Either the context or the concrete state objects are responsible for transitioning from one state to another.

The following class diagram shows how the behavior of an Amphicar might be modeled using the State design pattern.

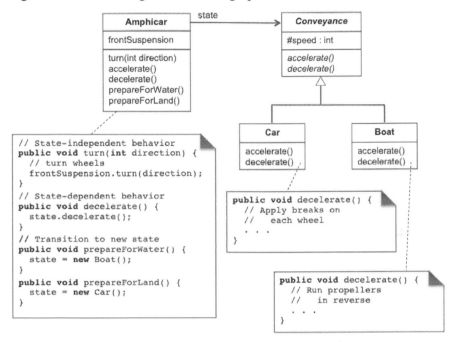

**Figure 55  Conceptual design for an Amphicar**

An Amphicar can be in one of two states: Car or Boat. An Amphicar's behavior depends on its current state. While on land, Amphicar will keep a reference to an instance of Car and act like a car. While on water, Amphicar will keep a reference to an instance of Boat and act like a boat.

Clients make certain requests of an Amphicar (ie turn(), accelerate(), decelerate()). State-dependent behavior such as accelerating and decelerating are forwarded to the object representing the current state. State-independent behaviors such as turning left and right are handled locally in Amphicar (remember, the front wheels of an Amphicar steer both on land and in the water).

# Sample Code

Imagine you have been asked to design the software for a simple cell phone with just 4 keys: SND, END, Side Key Up and Side Key Down.

Because cell phones have limited space for physical keys, the same keys are often mapped to different functions depending on the current state or mode of the phone (standby, talking, application running, etc.). For the phone in this example, assume the four keys are mapped to the following functions:

SND Key:          When in standby mode, this key will cause the phone to transition into call mode.

END Key:          When in call mode or application mode (running an application), this key will cause the phone to transition into standby mode.

Side Key
Up/Down:          When in standby mode, this key will raise or lower ringer volume. When in call mode, this key will raise or lower voice volume. When in application mode, this key will scroll the display up or down.

Based on the description, the phone appears to be an ideal candidate for the State design pattern. It has clearly identifiable states or modes and the behavior of certain keys depends on the current state of the phone.

One of the best ways to get a complete and accurate picture of the problem you are about to solve with the State design pattern is to model the proposed system with a state machine diagram. Figure 56 shows the state machine diagram for the proposed cell phone.

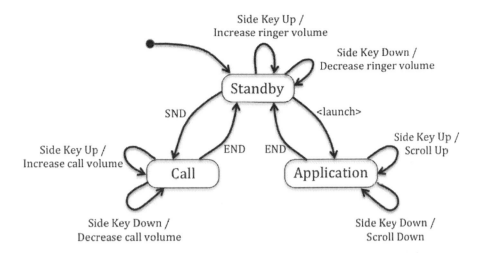

**Figure 56  State machine diagram for a cell phone**

The state machine diagram in Figure 56 shows the phone can be in one of three states: Standby, Call or Application. It also shows the events (labels on arrows) that trigger an activity (e.g. increase ringer volume) or cause a transition from one state to another.

Once you have a state machine diagram for a proposed application, transforming it into a design based on the State design pattern is straightforward.

Figure 57 shows the resulting class diagram for a software design based on the State diagram in Figure 56.

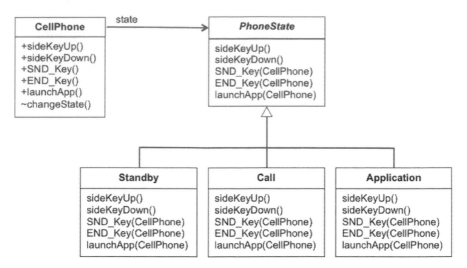

**Figure 57  Cell phone design based on the State design pattern**

The abstract class `PhoneState` defines an operation for each event in the state machine diagram. A separate concrete subclass is created for each state in the state machine diagram (Standby, Call and Application). These subclasses encapsulate state-specific behavior.

The following code shows the implementation details. In this particular example, state objects control the timing of state transitions. Changes in state are made by calling `CellPhone`'s `changeState()` operation.

```
public class StateExample {

    public static void main(String[] args) {
        CellPhone phone = new CellPhone();
        phone.sideKeyUp();
        phone.launchApp();
        phone.sideKeyUp();
        // Test error checking.
        // The following request is invalid
        //   for the current state
        phone.SND_Key();
        phone.END_Key();
        phone.sideKeyUp();
    }
}
```

```java
class CellPhone {
   private PhoneState state;

   public CellPhone() {
      state = new Standby();
   }

   public void sideKeyUp() {
      state.sideKeyUp();
   }

   public void sideKeyDown() {
      state.sideKeyDown();
   }

   public void SND_Key() {
      state.SND_Key(this);
   }

   public void END_Key() {
      state.END_Key(this);
   }

   public void launchApp() {
      state.launchApp(this);
   }

   // This method has package visibility.
   // Only internal classes can affect a
   //    change in the state of the context.
   void changeState(PhoneState state) {
      this.state = state;
   }
}

abstract class PhoneState {
   // Default behavior for all events is to
   //    signal an error.
   public void sideKeyUp() {
      System.out.println("Play Error Sound");
   }

   public void sideKeyDown() {
      System.out.println("Play Error Sound");
   }
```

```java
   // A reference to CellPhone is needed because
   //   this operation may request a state change.
   public void SND_Key(CellPhone phone) {
      System.out.println("Play Error Sound");
   }

   public void END_Key(CellPhone phone) {
      System.out.println("Play Error Sound");
   }

   public void launchApp(CellPhone phone) {
      System.out.println("Play Error Sound");
   }
}


// Concrete State
class Standby extends PhoneState {
   public void sideKeyUp() {
      System.out.println("Increase ringer volume");
   }

   public void sideKeyDown() {
      System.out.println("Decrease ringer volume");
   }

   public void SND_Key(CellPhone phone) {
      phone.changeState(new Call());
   }

   public void launchApp(CellPhone phone) {
      phone.changeState(new Application());
   }
}

class Call extends PhoneState {
   public void sideKeyUp() {
      System.out.println("Increase voice volume");
   }

   public void sideKeyDown() {
      System.out.println("Decrease voice volume");
   }

   public void END_Key(CellPhone phone) {
      phone.changeState(new Standby());
   }
}
```

```
class Application extends PhoneState {
   public void sideKeyUp() {
      System.out.println("Scroll up");
   }

   public void sideKeyDown() {
      System.out.println("Scroll down");
   }

   public void END_Key(CellPhone phone) {
      phone.changeState(new Standby());
   }
}
```

## Discussion

One issue to consider when applying the State design pattern is whether to make the context or individual state objects responsible for state transitions. If the criterion for transitioning between states is not a function of state, the most logical choice is to make the context responsible for state transitions. For example, in the implementation of Amphicar the context is responsible for switching between states because state transitions are state-independent. The transition from state A to state B doesn't depend on current state A.

In the cell phone example, individual state objects (subclasses of PhoneState) are responsible for state transitions. Putting state transition logic in state objects is reasonable for this application because state transitions occur as a consequence of receiving certain events while in certain states. For example, if the SND event is received while in the Standby state the Standby state object will transition the context to the Call state. Otherwise, the event is ignored. Doing the transition in the state object avoids state-checking conditional logic in the context object.

Allowing state objects to take responsibility for state transitions increases coupling between state objects (predecessor state must know about successor state) but generally results in code that is easier to understand and maintain.

## Related Patterns

State and Strategy have the same static structure (class diagrams) but differ in intent. The difference between the two patterns does, however, show up in their prototypical runtime behavior (sequence diagrams).

With State, clients have little or no knowledge of concrete state objects. The context typically decides the initial state and associated concrete state object. The context together with the state objects are responsible for transitions between states. State is also more dynamic with the context going through possibly many state changes during its lifetime.

With Strategy, clients are usually aware of different strategy objects and take responsibility for initializing the context with a specific strategy. Although clients can change a context's strategy at runtime, the configured strategy typically lasts for the lifetime of the context.

The Singleton design pattern can be used to create and manage state objects. If state classes are made Singleton classes, you don't have to create a new state object during every transition. Instead you can use the Instance() method of the state class to access the unique instance of the state class. For example:

```
public void launchApp(CellPhone phone) {
    phone.changeState(Application.Instance());
}
```

# Chapter 7  Strategy

In the context of the Strategy pattern, the term "strategy" is a synonym for algorithm or behavior.

## Introduction

Computer programs depend on algorithms. There are fundamental algorithms for routine activities like sorting and searching as well as application-specific algorithms for things like rating an insurance policy or calculating customer discounts.

Many times when programming you have a choice as to which algorithm to use to solve a problem. For example, there are more than 10 different mainstream algorithms for sorting a list of elements.

Algorithm selection is often a design time decision but there are times when it is necessary or desirable to postpone algorithm selection until runtime. Runtime selection is preferable when the choice of algorithm depends on factors not available at design time. Such factors include: nature of input, source of input, user preferences and current conditions. The following scenarios illustrate how these runtime factors can influence algorithm selection:

- In some situations detailed knowledge of input data can be used to select a more efficient algorithm at runtime. For example, insertion sort is likely to be faster than quicksort sort for a small number of input values. However, bucket sort outperforms both when variance among input values is low.
- Different validation algorithms might be used depending on whether the input data is coming from a trusted or untrusted source.
- User preference may directly affect algorithm choice. For example, selecting the economy mode on a hybrid car might activate a special algorithm for controlling throttle response and gear selection.
- A video game might switch from doing pixel-perfect collision detection to simply comparing the bounding box of images if performance (e.g. frames per second) drops below a certain threshold.

Components that postpone algorithm selection until runtime are good candidates for the Strategy design pattern. The Strategy design pattern shows how to design a class with interchangeable algorithms or behaviors.

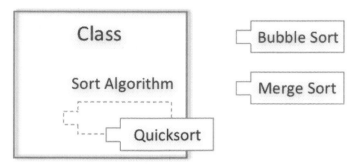

**Figure 58  The Strategy design pattern shows how to design a class with interchangeable algorithms**

# Intent

The Strategy design pattern defines a family of algorithms, encapsulates each one, and makes them interchangeable. Strategy lets the algorithm vary independently from clients that use it (Gamma 1995).

In practice, the opportunity to use the Strategy design pattern might show up as a class with mutually exclusive algorithms or behaviors that are selectable at runtime. For example, the following code fragment uses a compound if statement to select one of three algorithms:

```
class Context {
    void operation() {
        if ( . . .) {
            // algorithm 1
            . . .
        }
        else if ( . . .) {
            // algorithm 2
            . . .
        }
        else {
            // algorithm 3
            . . .
        }
    }
}
```

Strategy encapsulates each algorithm in a separate class and replaces the conditional logic in the context with delegation to an encapsulated algorithm.

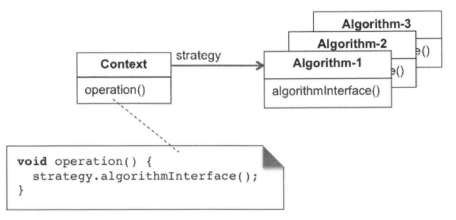

```
void operation() {
  strategy.algorithmInterface();
}
```

Separating the algorithms from the context allows the two to vary independently. New algorithms can be added or existing ones modified without altering the context. Conversely, the context can be modified without affecting the algorithms.

## Solution

Figure 59 shows the structure diagram for the Strategy design pattern.

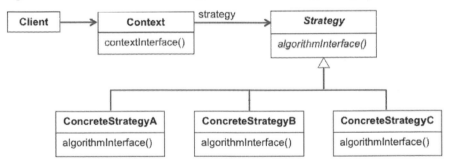

**Figure 59  Structure diagram for Strategy design pattern**

There is a concrete strategy class for each interchangeable algorithm or behavior. Note, in the context of the Strategy pattern, the term "strategy" is a synonym for algorithm or behavior.

Strategy defines an interface common to all concrete strategy classes. All concrete strategy classes must implement the same interface.

Context is a class with a configurable algorithm or behavior. It keeps a reference to a Strategy object, which is the abstract interface for a concrete strategy.

Clients usually choose which algorithm is used by the context:

```
void clientCode() {
    Strategy s = new ConcreteStrategyC();
    Context c = new Context(s);
}
```

The context delegates to the configured algorithm:

```
class Context {
    private Strategy strategy;

    // Constructor
    public Context(Strategy s) {
        strategy = s;
    }
    public void contextInterface() {
        . . .
        strategy.algorithmInterface();
        . . .
    }
}
```

## Sample Code

In statistics, a sample is a subset of a population. Oftentimes it is impractical to study every member of a population so a sample is selected for study. If it is a representative sample, the information gathered can be used to draw conclusions about the population as a whole.

There are several methods or algorithms for selecting a representative sample. The sample code in this section defines two such algorithms: RandomSample and SystematicSample. RandomSample picks n elements from the population at random. SystematicSample sorts the population and picks n elements at regular intervals from the sorted list.

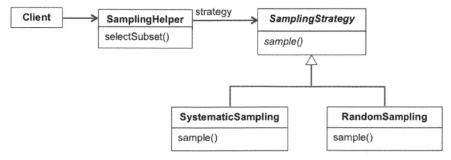

**Figure 60  UML class diagram for sample code**

The population in this example is an array of zip codes.
SamplingHelper is the context. The class Client creates and
configures SamplingHelper with an algorithm and then asks
SamplingHelper to select a subset. The selection process is done
according to the configured algorithm.

```java
import java.util.ArrayList;
import java.util.Arrays;
import java.util.Random;

public class Client {

    public static void main(String args[]) {

        // Population
        int[] zipCodes = new int[]
        {66209,64113,10162,90210,
        61701,55901,48823,62901,50014};

        // Instantiate an algorithm and use it to select
        a sample
        //   from the population
        SamplingStrategy strategy = new RandomSampling();
        SamplingHelper helper = new
        SamplingHelper(zipCodes,strategy);
        int[] sample = helper.selectSubset(3);

        // Output the sample
        for(int i=0; i<sample.length; i++)
            System.out.println(sample[i]);
        System.out.println();

        // Create another sample using a different
        algorithm
        strategy = new SystematicSampling();
        helper = new SamplingHelper(zipCodes,strategy);
        sample = helper.selectSubset(4);

        for(int i=0; i<sample.length; i++)
            System.out.println(sample[i]);
    }
}
```

```java
// Context
class SamplingHelper {
   private int[] population;
   private SamplingStrategy strategy;

   public SamplingHelper(int[] population,
   SamplingStrategy strategy) {
      this.population = population;
      this.strategy = strategy;
   }

   public int[] selectSubset(int sampleSize) {
      return strategy.sample(population, sampleSize);
   }
}

interface SamplingStrategy {
   int[] sample(int[] population, int sampleSize);
}

// Simple random sampling. Each element has an
//    equal probability of being selected.
class RandomSampling implements SamplingStrategy {
   public int[] sample(int[] population, int
   sampleSize) {
      int[] subset = new int[sampleSize];
      Random generator = new Random();

      // Using an ArrayList makes it easy to sample
      //    without replacement
      ArrayList<Integer> tempArray = new
      ArrayList<Integer>();

      for(int i=0; i<population.length; i++)
         tempArray.add(population[i]);

      for(int i=0; i<sampleSize; i++)
         subset[i] = tempArray.remove(
      generator.nextInt( tempArray.size() ));

      return subset;
   }
}
```

```
// Systematic sampling algorithm.
// Sort elements and then select elements at
//      regular intervals
class SystematicSampling implements SamplingStrategy {
    public int[] sample(int[] population, int
    sampleSize) {
        int[] subset = new int[sampleSize];
        Random generator = new Random();

        // Make a copy of the population array.
        // We don't want to cause function side effects.
        int[] sortedPopulation = new
        int[population.length];
        System.arraycopy(population, 0,
        sortedPopulation, 0, population.length);
        Arrays.sort(sortedPopulation);

        int step = sortedPopulation.length / sampleSize;
        int startingPoint = generator.nextInt(step+1);

        // select elements at regular interval 'step'
        for(int i=0; i<sampleSize; i++)
            subset[i] = sortedPopulation[startingPoint +
            (i*step)];

        return subset;
    }
}
```

## Discussion

One issue to consider when implementing the Strategy design pattern is how to handle data interchange between the context and strategy objects. One option is to have Context pass data via parameters when calling operations on strategy objects. This is the approached used in the example above:

```
// pass parameters population and sampleSize
strategy.sample(population, sampleSize);
```

Another option is to pass a reference to the context and have strategy objects use call back methods on the context to fetch needed data.

```
// pass a reference to the context
strategy.sample(this);
```

The first option is appropriate when all strategy objects share the same interface and there is small number of parameters. The second option is more appropriate when strategy objects have different data needs and/or extensive data needs. The one drawback of the second option is increased coupling. With the first option the context knows about strategy objects but strategy objects don't know about the context. With the second option there is a two-way dependency between context and strategy objects. The second option also requires data retrieval methods on the context. Adding additional data access methods to context goes against the principle of information hiding.

One of the drawbacks of the Strategy design pattern is clients must be aware of different strategy algorithms and understand the tradeoffs among the different algorithms in order to select the best one for a given situation. This increases coupling between clients and the details of implementation. One way to mitigate this drawback is to have the context configure a default strategy object or respond with default behavior when the client has configured no strategy object. Clients that don't know or don't care about strategy objects can use the default. Clients that do care about strategy objects can override the default behavior and install their own choice of strategy.

## Related Patterns

Strategy has the same static structure as State. The Related Patterns section of the State design pattern describes what is unique about each pattern.

# Chapter 8  Factory Method

Class inheritance and method overriding have long been used in object-oriented programming to change the behavior of a class. The Factory Method is a special case where the behavior changed is object creation.

## Introduction

The standard way of creating an object is to instantiate a concrete class directly with the new operator:

```
SomeClass sc = new SomeClass();
```

One of the drawbacks of using the new operator to create an object is the need to specify the type of object to create. Specifically, it creates a dependency between your code and the class or type of object created. Sometimes a more general solution is needed, one that allows control over when an instance of an object is created but leaves open or delegates to another class the specific type of object to create. Decoupling object creation from object use results in code that is more flexible and extendable.

To illustrate, consider the following class PaymentService. Notice that PaymentService creates an instance of and calls methods on FinancialTrustCCP, a third-party credit card processing service.

```
 1: public class PaymentService {
 2:     private final static String recipientID = "123-456-789";
 3:     // Third-party credit card processing service
 4:     private FinancialTrustCCP ccp;
 5:
 6:     public PaymentService() {
 7:         ccp = new FinancialTrustCCP();
 8:     }
 9:
10:     // Move funds from sender to recipient
11:     public void pay(String senderID, String amount) {
12:         boolean approved = ccp.post(senderID, recipientID, amount);
13:         if (approved)
14:             . . .
15:         else
16:             . . .
17:     }
18: }
```

PaymentService creates an instance of FinancialTrustCCP at line 7. This creates a dependency between the two classes that can lead to problems. For one, it is impossible to unit test PaymentService independent of FinancialTrustCCP. If FinancialTrustCCP is a third-party service connected to the global banking network, each test will create a transaction in the global banking network.

The current design also violates the open/closed principle. There is no way to extend the current solution to work with other credit card processing services without modifying the code.

These shortcomings in the design can be addressed by the Factory Method design pattern. The Factory Method design pattern delegates object creation to subclasses. Here is a new version of PaymentService where subclasses decide which concrete class for credit card processing to create:

```
 1: public class PaymentService {
 2:     private final static String recipientID = "123-456-789";
 3:     // Reference to generic credit card processing service
 4:     private CCPService ccp;
 5:
 6:     public PaymentService() {
 7:         // Use factory method createCCPService() to get a
 8:         //    reference to a credit card processing service
 9:         ccp = createCCPService();
10:     }
11:
12:     // Move funds from sender to recipient
13:     public void pay(String senderID, String amount) {
14:         boolean approved = ccp.post(senderID, recipientID, amount);
15:         if (approved)
16:             . . .
17:         else
18:             . . .
19:     }
20:
21:     // createCCPService is a factory method
22:     // The default behavior is to create an instance of
23:     //    FinancialTrustCCP, but subclasses can override
24:     //    the method to return instances of other services.
25:     protected CCPService createCCPService() {
26:         // Assume FinancialTrustCCP has been modified to
27:         //    implement interface CCPService
28:         return new FinancialTrustCCP();
29:     }
30: }
31:
32: interface CCPService {
33:     boolean post(String senderID, String recipientID, String amount);
34: }
```

The new design is more flexible. It decouples object creation from object use. The class PaymentService delegates responsibility for creating an instance of a credit card processing service to the factory method createCCPService(). PaymentService provides a default implementation of createCCPService() but subclasses of PaymentService can override createCCPService() and substitute a different service. One practical benefit is test cases can

substitute a mock object in place of the live credit card processing service
`FinancialTrustCCP`. Here is an example test case that substitutes
mock object `MockCCPService` for `FinancialTrustCCP`:

```
 1: public class PaymentServiceTestRunner {
 2:
 3:     public static void main(String[] args) {
 4:         PaymentService ps = new PaymentServiceTest();
 5:         ps.pay("2121964", "50.00");
 6:         // Make sure PaymentService is in the correct state
 7:         //    after the credit card transaction was declined
 8:         assert . . .;
 9:     }
10: }
11:
12: class PaymentServiceTest extends PaymentService {
13:     protected CCPService createCCPService() {
14:         return new MockCCPService();
15:     }
16: }
17:
18: class MockCCPService implements CCPService {
19:     public boolean post(String senderID, String recipientID,
20:                         String amount) {
21:         // Decline credit request
22:         return false;
23:     }
24: }
```

The Factory Method is one of several creational patterns. It uses
inheritance and polymorphic methods to delegate responsibility for object
creation to subclasses. Class inheritance and method overriding have long
been used in object-oriented programming to change the behavior of a
class. The Factory Method is a special case where the behavior changed is
object creation.

## Intent

One of the most important rules-of-thumb in software design is, "program
to an interface, not an implementation". This advice is probably most
familiar in the context of calling operations on objects. You could write
client code that accepts a `LinkedList`:

```
void clientCodeA(LinkedList list) {
    for (int i=0; i < list.size(); i++)
        . . .
}
```

However, if there is nothing about `clientCodeA()` that requires a `LinkedList`, it is usually better to program to a more abstract interface supported by various concrete collection classes:

```
void clientCodeB(Collection collection) {
    for (int i=0; i < collection.size(); i++)
        . . .
}
```

`ClientCodeB()` is better than `clientCodeA()` because `clientCodeB()` works with any concrete type that conforms to the abstraction `Collection`. `clientCodeA()` only works for LinkedLists.

The advice "program to an interface, not an implementation" also applies to object creation. You could create an object with the `new` operator:

```
1:  class clientCodeC {
2:      public clientCodeC() {
3:          SupportingClass sc = new SupportingClass();
4:      }
5:  }
```

However, the reference to concrete class `SupportingClass` at line 3 is an example of programming to an implementation. If there is nothing about `clientCodeC` that requires an instance of `SupportingClass`, it is usually better to program to an abstract interface that will result in the creation of an instance of `SupportingClass` or another type that is compatible with the client code.

What's not so obvious is how to program to an interface when creating objects. That is precisely the problem solved by the Factory Method design pattern. The Factory Method Pattern "defines an interface for creating an object, but lets subclasses decide which class to instantiate. Factory Method lets a class defer instantiation to subclasses" (Gamma 1995).

Here is one way of redesigning the previous code fragment to use the Factory Method design pattern:

```
 1: class ClientCodeD {
 2:     public ClientCodeD() {
 3:         AbstractSupportingClass sc = createSupportingClass();
 4:     }
 5:     // Factory Method
 6:     protected AbstractSupportingClass createSupportingClass() {
 7:         . . .
 8:     }
 9: }
10: interface AbstractSupportingClass {
11:     . . .
12: }
```

In the revised code fragment, the overridable method createSupportingClass() is responsible for creating the object used at line 3. To change the type of object created at line 3 you would extend ClientCodeD and override createSupportingClass().

Notice that the revised solution also conforms to the open/closed principle. It is open for extension but closed for modification. You can change the type of object created at line 3 without altering the source code of ClientCodeD.

## Solution

The Factory Method design pattern has four main components (see Figure 60). The class Creator declares a factory method createProduct(). createProduct() returns an object of type Product. Subclasses of Creator (ConcreteCreator in Figure 61) override the factory method to create and return a concrete instance of Product (ConcreteProduct in Figure 61).

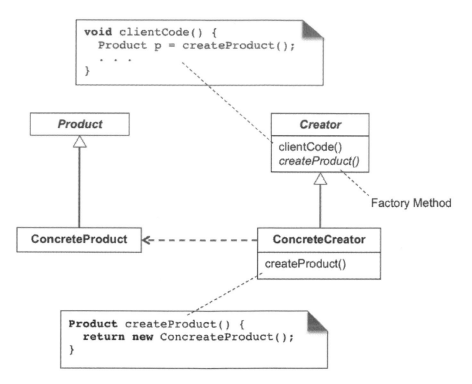

**Figure 61  Factory Method design pattern**

The client code that calls the factory method and manipulates products (through the abstract interface Product) is usually contained in Creator. However, this isn't a requirement of the design pattern. Client code may also reside outside the class with the factory method.

# Sample Code

### Example #1

Consider a hierarchy of classes for managing digital images where there is an abstract superclass Image that encapsulates features common to all image types and concrete subclasses for different image formats such as JPGImage for JPG images, PNGImage for PNG images, etc. Concrete subclasses contain logic for reading and writing image data for the image type they represent.

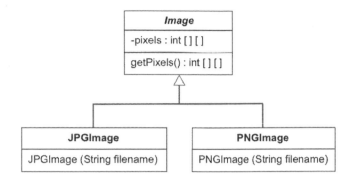

Given a file for one of the supported image types, you have to decide which concrete image class to instantiate (JPGImage or PNGImage). One option is to examine the filename suffix and hope it is appropriate for the file data. Another option is to examine the actual file data and look for the signatures of the different file formats in header data. This example shows how to organize such class creation logic using the Factory Method design pattern.

The example has two concrete product types (JPGImage and PNGImage) and two concrete creator types (ImageCreatorUsingFileExtensions and ImageCreatorUsingFileData):

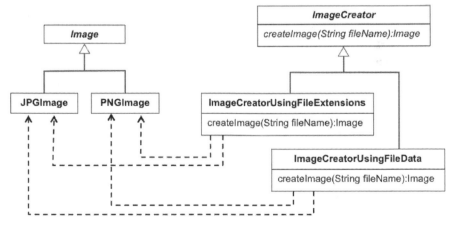

**Figure 62  One-to-many relationship between concrete creators and concrete products**

createImage(String fileName) is the factory method. Notice that it is parameterized. The parameter is used to decide which concrete

product to return. It takes the file name of the image and returns one of the
concrete product types.

```
class Client {
    public static void main(String[ ] args) {
        // Create an instance of a concrete creator.
        ImageCreator imageCreator = new
        ImageCreatorUsingFileExtensions();
        clientCode(imageCreator);
    }

    static void clientCode(ImageCreator imageCreator) {
        Image image1 =
        imageCreator.createImage("beach.jpg");
        Image image2 =
        imageCreator.createImage("sunset.png");
        // Process the images . . .
    }
}

abstract class ImageCreator {
    public abstract Image createImage(String fileName);

}

class ImageCreatorUsingFileExtensions extends
ImageCreator {
    public Image createImage(String fileName) {
        if (fileName.endsWith("jpg"))
            return new JPGImage(fileName);
        else if (fileName.endsWith("png"))
            return new PNGImage(fileName);
        else
            return null;
    }
}

class ImageCreatorUsingFileData extends ImageCreator {
    public Image createImage(String fileName) {
        // Use file data to decide image type
        . . .
    }
}
```

```
abstract class Image {
   private int [ ] [ ] pixels;

   public int [ ][ ] getPixels() {
      return pixels;
   }
}

class JPGImage extends Image {
   public JPGImage(String fileName) {
      // Read image data from fileName
      //    and store in pixels matrix.
      .  .  .
   }
}

class PNGImage extends Image {
   public PNGImage(String fileName) {
      // Read image data from fileName
      //    and store in pixels matrix.
      .  .  .
   }
}
```

## Example #2

Iteration in Java depends on the Factory Method design pattern. To see how, consider the following boilerplate code for iterating over the elements of a collection in Java:

```
1: void clientCode(Collection c) {
2:     Iterator i = c.iterator();   // iterator() is a Factory Method
3:     while (i.hasNext()) {
4:         .  .  .
5:     }
6: }
```

Line 2 includes a call to iterator(), which is a factory method defined for the interface Collection. Concrete collection classes decide which concrete iterator to create and return.

Figure 63 shows the structure diagram for iteration in Java. Notice how it differs from the structure diagram in the previous example (Figure 62). In the previous example there is a one-to-many relationship between concrete creators and concrete products. With iteration in Java there is a one-to-one relationship between concrete collection classes and concrete iterators. Both are valid forms of the pattern.

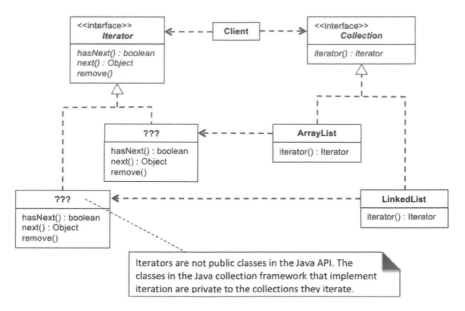

**Figure 63  Parallel class hierarchy for iteration in Java**

## Discussion

Most language libraries include a number of factory classes. I did a quick search of the javax package (a small subset of the JDK) and found 44 classes with the word "factory" in their name:

```
[burrise@babbage src]$ find javax -iname *factory*
javax/security/sasl/SaslClientFactory.java
javax/security/sasl/SaslServerFactory.java
javax/management/MBeanServerFactory.java
javax/management/remote/JMXConnectorServerFactory.java
javax/management/remote/JMXConnectorFactory.java
javax/swing/BorderFactory.java
. . .
```

What's interesting is only a small number of these self-described factory classes use the Factory Method design pattern. Many of the classes found (and others such as `java.util.Collections` that create objects but don't include the word "factory" in their name) create objects using simpler techniques that don't offer all the flexibility of the Factory Method pattern. A few definitions should help clarify the difference between the Factory Method pattern and these other techniques for creating objects.

A factory class is any class with one or more creational methods. A creational method is any method that returns an object. The Factory Method design pattern describes a class with a creational method that:

1.  is nonstatic
2.  is virtual (can be overridden)
3.  returns a base class or interface type

Factory Method is one type of creational method. All Factory Methods are creational methods but not all creational methods are Factory Methods.

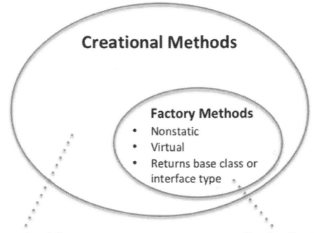

Factory Method, as described in (Gamma, et al. 1995), is a design pattern. The other techniques for creating objects are better thought of as programming idioms.

What are these other techniques for creating objects? A common programming idiom for creating objects is to use a static factory method in place of a constructor. For example, Java's Boolean class offers the static factory method valueOf(boolean b):

```
public class Boolean {
   public static final Boolean TRUE = new
   Boolean(true);
   public static final Boolean FALSE = new
   Boolean(false);
   . . .
   // Static factory method
   public static Boolean valueOf(boolean b) {
      return (b ? TRUE : FALSE);
   }
}
```

A static factory method is a public static method that returns an instance of its containing class. Clients needing an instance of the wrapper class

`Boolean` can call `valueOf(boolean b)` rather than one of `Boolean`'s constructors. The main advantages of using static factory methods in place of constructors are:

1.  More descriptive names. In most programming languages, constructor names must be the same as the class name. This constraint doesn't apply to static factory methods. They can be named to reflect their intent.
2.  More control over object creation. With static factory methods a new object doesn't have to be created each time the method is called. Immutable objects (e.g. `Boolean`) can be shared and mutable objects can be managed as a pool of reusable objects. Notice that the Singleton design pattern is essentially a static factory method where the policy is to create and reuse a single instance of the class.

Another programming idiom for creating objects is to define a factory class that does nothing but create objects. For example, all the methods defined for the class `javax.swing.BorderFactory` are dedicated to creating Border objects:

```
public class BorderFactory {
    public static Border createLineBorder(Color color) {
        . . .
    }
    public static Border createRaisedBevelBorder() {
        . . .
    }
    . . .
}
```

For added flexibility, the static methods of a dedicated factory class may return a base class or interface type. For example, `Border` is an interface. Clients of `BorderFactory` are unaware of (and therefore loosely coupled to) the concrete type of object returned.

## Related Patterns

Factory Method and Singleton are both creational patterns. The Singleton design pattern controls the number of instances of a class that are created. The Factory Method design pattern decouples object creation from object use.

The Iterator design pattern uses a factory method to return the appropriate concrete iterator.

Factory methods are often used with Template Methods. The Template Method design pattern defers steps in an algorithm to subclasses. One of the steps typically is object creation.

# Chapter 9  Observer

## Introduction

Designing software as a loose confederation of cooperating objects often brings with it the need to maintain consistency between related objects (Gamma, et al. 1995). For example, consider an integrated development environment (IDE) with multiple views of the underlying source code. Most IDE's offer an edit window along with other views such as an outline view and a type hierarchy.

Views or Observers

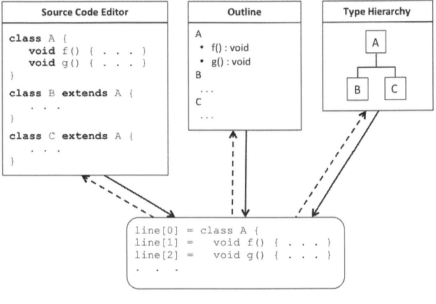

Subject

**Figure 64  IDE with multiple views of source code**

A change to the underlying data through one of the views is immediately reflected in the other views that are visible. One way to implement this is to locate everything in one large tightly coupled class. This is a poor design choice though because it makes it impossible to reuse the views or the data structure independently. It also complicates maintenance. Adding a new view would require modifying the existing class.

A better design is one that organizes the views and underlying data structure into separate loosely coupled cooperating objects. This facilitates reuse and extension but also creates the problem of how to keep the views in sync with the underlying data. One option is to have view objects repeatedly poll the underlying data structure for changes. This would be a waste of resources though because in most cases there would be no changes. A more efficient solution is to use the Observer design pattern.

With the Observer design pattern a subject object (the underlying data structure in this example) keeps a list of observers (views in this example). When the state of the subject changes, observers are notified and given a chance to synchronize with the subject.

## Intent

The Observer design pattern defines a one-to-many relationship between a subject object and any number of observer objects such that when the subject object changes, observer objects are notified and given a chance to react to changes in the subject.

## Solution

The three main components of the Observer design pattern are: Subject, Observer and ConcreteObserver.

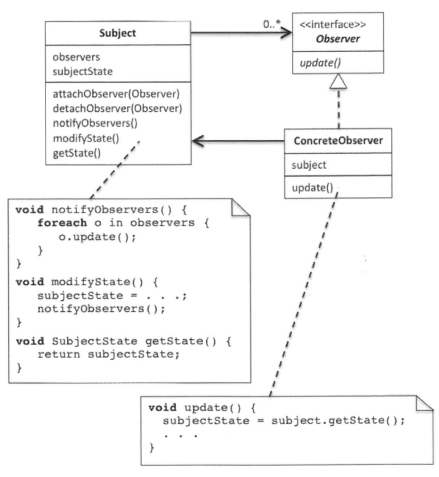

**Figure 65  Static structure for Observer design pattern**

The Subject is responsible for:

- Attaching and detaching observers
- Notifying attached observers when the state of the subject changes
- Application-specific state and logic

Observer defines an abstract interface with the callback operation subject objects use to notify observers of a change. A subject is loosely coupled to its observers because the subject only knows about its observers through the abstract interface Observer.

ConcreteObserver implements the abstract interface Observer. ConcreteObserver may keep a reference to the Subject it is observing. (The other option is to pass a reference to the subject on the update() method.)

The reference to the subject is used to query the subject for more details when notified of a change in the state of the subject.

The pseudo code in the UML static diagram above gives some indication of the dynamic interaction between components. The following sequence diagram clarifies typical interaction by showing the order of operations for one scenario of use.

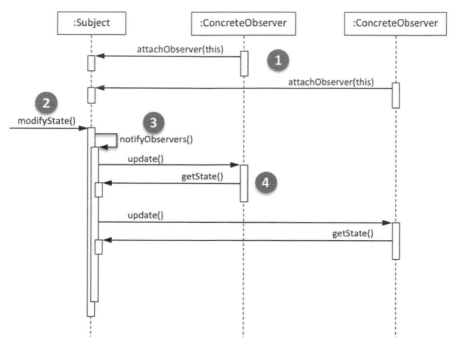

**Figure 66  Dynamic interactions in Observer design pattern**

(1) During the setup phase observers are registered with the subject. Observers may attach themselves or be added to the subject via a third party.

(2) A change in the state of the subject may be initiated from a third party or one of the views.

(3) After a change in the state of the subject, the subject will notify registered observers. The sequence diagram above shows notifyObservers() being called from within the subject at the end of a state-modifying operation. In some cases, though, it may be more efficient to let clients decide when notifyObservers() is called. For example, if a client plans to make several changes to a data structure representing an on screen object, it might be more efficient to have clients call notifyObservers() after calling a series of state-changing operations on the subject data

structure. Having the subject call notifyObservers() after every state-changing operation simplifies the design from the client's perspective but also may result in unnecessary intermediate updates.

(4) When notified of a change in the subject, observers may query the subject for the details of what has changed (the pull method). Another option is for subjects to forward information about the change to observers through the update method (the push method). The push method is probably more efficient but it increases the coupling from subject to observers making it harder to reuse observers in other contexts.

Logic in the subject for attaching, detaching and notifying observers is the same for all subjects. One way to avoid repeating this logic in different subjects is to encapsulate the logic in a separate reusable class Subject that is inherited by all concrete subjects.

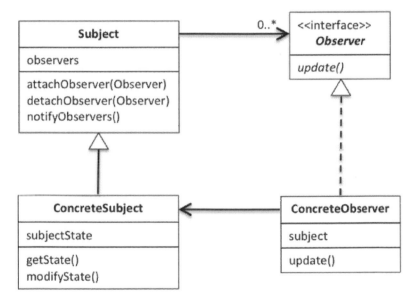

**Figure 67 Alternate organization for Observer design pattern**

# Sample Code

The Java program in this section has one subject with two observers. The subject is Stock, a class that encapsulates the name and price of a stock. One of the observers is StockView, a class that prints the current symbol and price of the stock it is observing. The other observer is StockTrader, a class that watches the price of a stock and sells when the stock reaches a certain price.

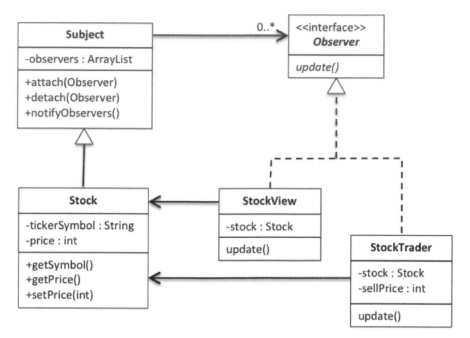

**Figure 68  Class diagram for sample code**

The following code creates an instance of a stock with two observers and then changes the price of the stock three times.

```java
import java.util.ArrayList;

public class ObserverRunner {
    public static void main(String[] args) {
        Stock stock = new Stock("IBM",250);
        StockView sv = new StockView(stock);
        StockTrader st = new StockTrader(stock,253);

        stock.setPrice(251);
        stock.setPrice(252);
        stock.setPrice(253);
    }
}

interface Observer {
    void update();
}
```

```java
class Subject {
   private ArrayList observers = new ArrayList();

   public void attach(Observer o) {
      observers.add(o);
   }

   public void detach(Observer o) {
      observers.remove(o);
   }

   public void notifyObservers() {
      for (Object o : observers) {
         Observer observer = (Observer)o;
         observer.update();
      }
   }
}

class Stock extends Subject {
   private String tickerSymbol;
   private int price;

   public Stock(String tickerSymbol, int price) {
      this.tickerSymbol = tickerSymbol;
      this.price = price;
   }

   public String getSymbol() {
      return tickerSymbol;
   }

   public int getPrice() {
      return price;
   }

   public void setPrice(int price) {
      this.price = price;
      notifyObservers();
   }
}
```

```java
class StockView implements Observer {
   private Stock stock;

   public StockView(Stock stock) {
      this.stock = stock;
      stock.attach(this);
   }

   public void update() {
      System.out.println(stock.getSymbol() +
      " is selling for " + stock.getPrice());
   }
}

class StockTrader implements Observer {
   private Stock stock;
   private int sellPrice;

   public StockTrader(Stock stock, int sellPrice) {
      this.stock = stock;
      this.sellPrice = sellPrice;
      stock.attach(this);
   }

   public void update() {
      if (stock.getPrice() >= sellPrice)
         System.out.println("Sell " + stock.getSymbol()
         + "!");
   }
}
```

The output of the program above is:

```
IBM is selling for 251
IBM is selling for 252
IBM is selling for 253
Sell IBM!
```

## Discussion

The example in the previous section used the Observer design pattern without any help from the Java Class Library. Java, like many other languages, provides a framework in its standard library for implementing the Observer design pattern. It defines a class Observable and an interface Observer.

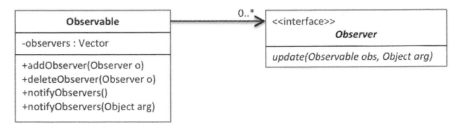

**Figure 69  Java's support for the Observer design pattern**

Subject and Observer in the previous example can be replaced by Observerable and Observer from the Java Class Library, saving more than 20 lines of code.

Java's framework for implementing the Observer design pattern also shows how the pattern can be extended to support both the push and pull methods of update discussed earlier. The class Observable has two methods for notifying observers:

```
notifyObservers()
notifyObservers(Object arg)
```

The first method notifies observers without any extra information about the change in the state of the subject. The second method is used to push state changes directly to observers. The value passed arrives at observers as the second parameter on the callback method update(Observerable obs, Object arg). When the first method is used to notify observers the second parameter on the callback method is null.

The first parameter on the callback method update() points out another variation on the Observer design pattern. Observers observing multiple subjects need some why of identifying the source of a notification. The first parameter of the update method is a reference to the Observable object calling the update method. Here is an example of how observers might use this parameter to distinguish between updates coming from multiple subjects.

```
class ConcreteObserver implements Observer {
   Observable subject1;
   Observable subject2;
   . . .
   public void update(Observerable obs, Object arg) {
      if (obs == subject1) {
         . . .
      } else if (obs == subject2) {
         . . .
      }
   }
}
```

## Related Patterns

The Observer design pattern is used in the Model-View-Controller architecture. The data model is the subject and views are observers.

# Chapter 10  Façade

## Introduction

If you believe the old adage "There's no problem in Computer Science that can't be solved by adding another layer of abstraction to it." you are going to like the Façade design pattern. The Façade design pattern adds another layer of abstraction to a complex or poorly designed subsystem.

A good example of the Façade design pattern is the JOptionPane class in the Java Class Library. JOptionPane simplifies and unifies the low level interface for creating dialog boxes in Java.

To appreciate the benefits of using JOptionPane to create dialog boxes, consider the amount of code needed to create and show a simple dialog box using the base Swing classes in the Java Class Library:

```java
JPanel panel = new JPanel();
JLabel messageLabel =
    new JLabel("Press OK to continue.");
JButton OKButton = new JButton("OK");
final JDialog customDialog = new JDialog();
panel.add(messageLabel);
panel.add(OKButton);
customDialog.getContentPane().add(
    panel,BorderLayout.CENTER);
customDialog.pack();

OKButton.addActionListener(new ActionListener(){
    public void actionPerformed(ActionEvent e){
        customDialog.dispose();
    }
});
customDialog.setVisible(true);
```

For all the effort, the result is a rather plain looking dialog box:

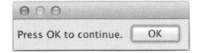

Compare the code above to what is required when using JOptionPane to create and show a similar dialog box:

```java
JOptionPane.showMessageDialog(
    null,"Press OK to continue.");
```

It takes just one line of code to create a dialog box with `JOptionPane`. The code is simple and the resulting dialog box has a standard look and feel that is much more visually appealing than the handcrafted one:

`JOptionPane` is a Façade class. A Façade class simplifies and unifies access to a larger more complex set of classes belonging to some subsystem. `JOptionPane` simplifies access to the Java subsystem for creating and showing dialog boxes. `JOptionPane` doesn't do any of the heavy lifting of creating dialog boxes. The operations on `JOptionPane` simply delegate requests to existing classes.

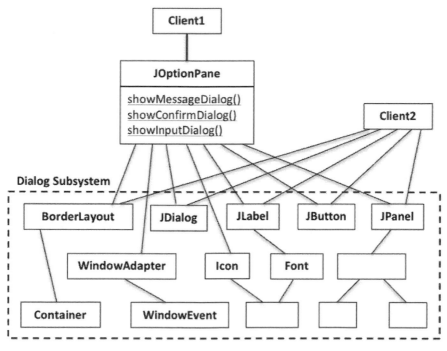

**Figure 70  JOptionPane Façade**

Notice also from Figure 70 that JOptionPane doesn't encapsulate the low-level support for creating dialog boxes. Clients are free to go around JOptionPane and create dialog boxes directly using the primitive support provided in the Java Class Library. However, it's better to go through JOptionPane for standard dialog boxes because it simplifies client code and makes it easier to enforce a standard look and feel.

## Intent

The intent of the Façade design pattern is to "provide a unified interface to a set of interfaces in a subsystem. Façade defines a higher-level interface that makes the subsystem easier to use" (Gamma 1995).

There are three benefits to using the Façade design pattern:

1. **Unification**. A Façade class defines a single point of access for clients. Clients deal with one class as opposed to a large interface or complex set of interfaces.
2. **Abstraction and simplification**. The interface offered by the Façade class is a level of abstraction above that of the wrapped interface. This simplifies client code.
3. **Decreased coupling**. A Façade class decouples clients from the details of a subsystem. Clients that access the services of a subsystem through a Façade class are buffered from changes in the subsystem.

## Solution

The Façade design pattern is one of the easiest to understand and implement. It doesn't use inheritance or polymorphism and there are no interfaces to implement. It takes only one class to implement the Façade design pattern. The class includes operations that provide a high-level interface onto an existing subsystem. The operations are implemented by delegating to lower-level components (usually classes) in the existing subsystem.

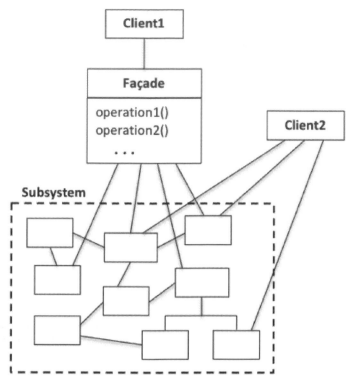

**Figure 71  Façade design pattern**

A Façade class doesn't encapsulate, but rather, "wraps" an existing subsystem. "Wraps" is a better term for the relationship because clients are free to go around the Façade and access the features of the subsystem directly.

# Sample Code

The sample code in this section uses the metaphor of a camera to show how much easier it is to take a picture when there is a façade class that wraps the raw camera controls. The PointAndShootFaçade, like a point and shoot camera, hides the complexity of the low-level camera interface, which includes a light meter and controls for shutter speed and aperture size. The PointAndShootFaçade doesn't offer all the flexibility of the low-level interface but it is much easier to use when all you want to do is simply take a picture.

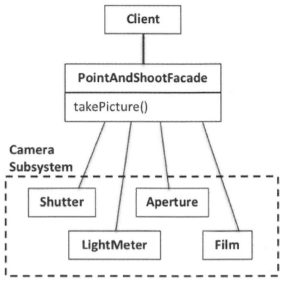

**Figure 72  Class diagram for code sample**

The low-level camera interface includes controls for shutter speed and aperture size along with a light meter service class and film component. The static method `client1()` takes a picture using `PointAndShootFacade`. The static method `client2()` takes a picture using the low-level camera interface. Notice how much simpler the code is for `client1()` compared to `client2()`.

```
public class Client {
    public static void main(String[] args) {
        client1();
        client2();
    }

    // client1 takes a picture using
    PointAndShootFacade.
    public static void client1() {
        PointAndShootFacade pointAndShootCamera =
        new PointAndShootFacade();
        pointAndShootCamera.takePicture();
    }
```

```
   // client2 takes a picture using the raw camera
   interface.
   public static void client2() {
      Shutter shutter = new Shutter();
      Aperture aperture = new Aperture();
      Film film = new Film();

      // Clients that don't use the Facade interface
      are
      //    forced to understand the subtle tradeoffs
      //    between film speed, shutter speed and
      aperture size.
      int filmSpeed = film.getFilmSpeed();
      if (filmSpeed <= 200) {
         shutter.setSpeed(1.0/30.0);
         aperture.setSize(5.6);
      }
      else if (filmSpeed >= 400) {
         shutter.setSpeed(1.0/60.0);
         aperture.setSize(8);
      }
      else {
         shutter.setSpeed(1.0/45.0);
         aperture.setSize(5.6);
      }

      shutter.trigger();
   }
}

class PointAndShootFacade {
   private Shutter shutter;
   private Aperture aperture;
   private Film film;

   public PointAndShootFacade() {
      shutter = new Shutter();
      aperture = new Aperture();
      film = new Film();
   }
```

```java
    public void takePicture() {
        LightMeter lightMeter = new
        LightMeter(film.getFilmSpeed());
        shutter.setSpeed(lightMeter.getRecommendedShutter
        Speed());
        aperture.setSize(lightMeter.getRecommendedApertur
        eSize());
        shutter.trigger(); // take the picture
    }
}

class Shutter {
    private double speed;

    public void setSpeed(double speed) {
        this.speed = speed;
    }

    public void trigger() {
        System.out.format("Open shutter for %.3f
        seconds\n", speed);
    }
}

class Aperture {
    private double size;

    public void setSize(double size) {
        this.size = size;
    }
}

class Film {
    public int getFilmSpeed() {
        return 200;  // hard coded for this example
    }
}
```

```
class LightMeter {
   private int filmSpeed;

   public LightMeter(int filmSpeed) {
      this.filmSpeed = filmSpeed;
   }

   public double getRecommendedShutterSpeed() {
      return 1.0/60.0; // hard coded for this example
   }

   public double getRecommendedApertureSize() {
      return 5.6; // hard coded for this example

   }
}
```

Output:

```
Open shutter for 0.017 seconds
Open shutter for 0.033 seconds
```

## Discussion

The Façade design pattern is often used with the layered architecture style. One way to reduce coupling between layers is to have clients access the services of a layer through one or more Façade classes. The more components there are within a layer the greater the benefit of having a few well-defined access points.

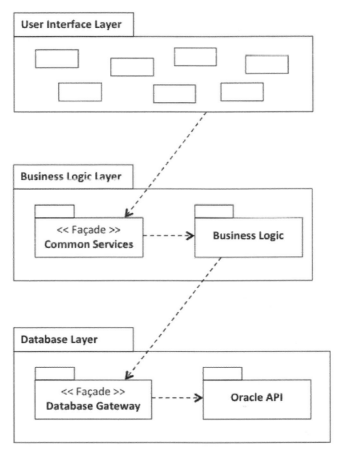

**Figure 73  Façade design pattern being used with the layered architecture style**

Architectural patterns Table Data Gateway and Row Data Gateway are special cases of the Façade design pattern. They encapsulate the details of accessing the underlying database.

# Related Patterns

The Façade design pattern uses object composition and delegation, as do other design patterns such as Adapter, Bridge, Proxy and Decorator. See Related Patterns under Adapter for the distinction between these structurally similar patterns.

# Chapter 11  Template Method

## Introduction

Joe Johnson, lead foreman at Peak Roofing, was asked by his boss to prepare written procedures for performing their company's signature service: roof replacement. Joe quickly concluded that it would be impractical to create just one set of procedures, as different customers had different priorities. For example, some customers were price sensitive while others were more concerned with the quality of the work.

To get started, Joe decided to write two separate procedure manuals, one for replacing a roof at minimal cost and another for replacing a roof when quality was the first priority.

Here is the result:

### Cheap Roof Replacement

Step 1: *Prepare jobsite*. Secure safe access to roof.

Step 2: *Prepare surface for new roof*. If there is only one layer of existing roof shingles, leave them on. Otherwise, remove all existing layers.

Step 3: *Install new roof*.

Step 4: *Clean jobsite*. If there is any roofing debris around the perimeter of the house, till it into the soil or sweep it under the porch when the homeowner isn't looking.


### Quality Roof Replacement

Step 1: *Prepare jobsite*. Secure safe access to roof. Cover plants around the perimeter of the house.

Step 2: *Prepare surface for new roof*. Remove all existing layers of roofing shingles. Add membrane to prevent ice dams.

Step 3: *Install new roof*.

Step 4: *Clean jobsite*. Remove plant covers and any remaining debris around the perimeter of the house.


One concern with having two manuals is the overlap between the two procedures. They both share the same steps, and some steps include the same activities. Keeping both documents consistent and up-to-date is going to be a challenge.

As you might expect, this is a problem for which the Template Method design pattern is ideally suited. The Template Method design pattern shows how to represent an algorithm with customizable steps in a way that reduced redundancy. The problem presented here is analogous. The algorithm or basic steps for replacing a roof is the same whether the goal is to minimize cost or maximize quality. Only the detailed activities within the steps are different.

Figure 74 shows how the problem presented here can be solved with the Template Method design pattern. The invariant parts of the procedure are declared in an abstract base class. The variant parts are declared in subclasses. The sequence of steps for replacing a roof are defined in the template method `replaceRoof()`. Subclasses—one for each type of roof replacement—override methods called from `replaceRoof()` to implement variations on the basic procedure.

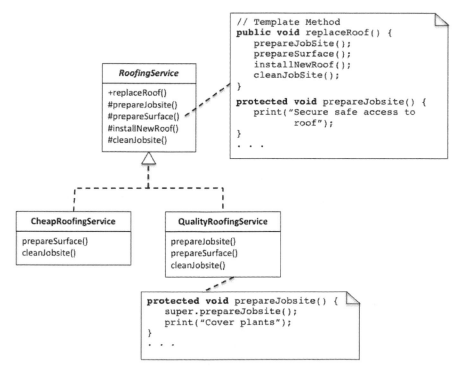

**Figure 74  Conceptual example of Template Method design pattern**

Client code for the above design would look something like:

```
QualityRoofingService service =
   new QualityRoofingService();
service.replaceRoof();
```

## Intent

One indication there is an opportunity to improve existing code with the Template Method design pattern is having two or more procedures or code fragments with the same basic structure but different detailed steps. For example, imagine finding the following two procedures in a program:

```
void growTomatoes () {
   digHole();
   plantSeeds();
   if (isWarmClimate())
      mulch();
   while (! frost())
      water();
}

void growPumpkins () {
   digHole();
   plantSeeds();
   while (! frost()) {
      water();
      prune();
   }
}
```

After reading through both procedures it is clear something is being duplicated, but exactly what might not be immediately obvious. The procedures are similar but not duplicates of each other. You simply can't replace one with the other because the details of each are different.

What is being duplicated here is the structure of the algorithm for growing flowering plants. If in the future you wanted to add say a harvest() function, you would have to update the growing procedures for all flowering plants, even if the harvest() function was the same for all plants.

Duplicate code complicates maintenance and increases the risk of introducing bugs when making changes. It is important to be able to recognize duplication and understand how to eliminate it in whatever form it may take. The Template Method design pattern shows how to eliminate repetition in algorithm structure.

With the Template Method design pattern the structure of an algorithm is represented once with variations on the algorithm implemented by subclasses. The skeleton of the algorithm is declared in a template method in terms of overridable operations. Subclasses are allowed to extend or replace some or all of these operations.

## Solution

With the Template Method design pattern, an algorithm is broken down into primitive operations. The skeleton of the algorithm is defined in a template method that resides in an abstract base class. Concrete subclasses implement variations on the algorithm by overriding specific operations.

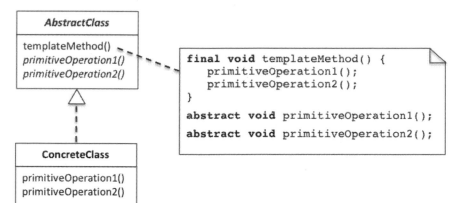

**Figure 75  Template Method design pattern**

There are three different types of operations called from template methods:

```
public abstract class AbstractClass {
    public final void templateMethod() {
        operation1();
        operation2();
        operation3();
    }

    protected abstract void operation1();

    protected void operation2() {
        // hook operations are defined with
        //    empty or default implementation
    }

    protected final void operation3() {
        // algorithm behavior that can't
        //    be changed
        . . .
    }
}
```

1. Abstract operations declared in the base class that subclasses *must* define.

2. Concrete operations defined in the base class that subclasses *may* redefine. These methods are called hook methods because they give subclasses the ability to "hook into" the algorithm at various points. Hook operations are given empty or default implementation.

3. Invariant operations. The algorithm may include steps that must be included in all instances of the algorithm. Operations that are invariant are declared non-polymorphic (final in Java; sealed in C#) to prevent subclasses from overriding them.

## Sample Code

The example in this section shows how to restructure `growTomatoes()` and `growPumpkins()` to use the Template Method design pattern.

Recall the similarity between the two procedures:

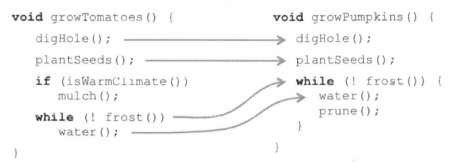

```
void growTomatoes() {            void growPumpkins() {
    digHole();                       digHole();
    plantSeeds();                    plantSeeds();
    if (isWarmClimate())             while (! frost()) {
        mulch();                         water();
    while (! frost())                    prune();
        water();                     }
}                                }
```

Analyzing the individual steps we can extract the general algorithm for growing a vegetable:

```
void growVegetable() {
    digHole();
    plantSeeds();
    mulch();
    while (!frost()) {
        water();
        prune();
    }
}
```

Actions such as `mulch()` and `prune()`, which are applicable to some but not all vegetables, are included in the general algorithm. Subclasses will have the chance to ignore or override the behavior of these operations.

The next step is to decide how to declare each method called from the template method. Methods may be declared as: (1) abstract, (2) concrete with default implementation, (3) concrete with empty implementation, and (4) non-polymorphic.

The following guidelines were used in the design of this example:

1. Methods expected to have unique implementation in most subclasses were declared abstract.
2. Methods expected to share the same implementation in many subclasses were declared concrete and given default implementation.

3.  Methods needed for only a small fraction of subclasses were declared concrete and given empty implementation.
4.  Methods representing invariant steps in the algorithm were declared non-polymorphic. If the method might be useful to a subclass, it was declared protected. Otherwise, it was declared private.

Here is the complete program:

```
abstract class Vegetable {

    // helper class used to consolidate weather
    //      information
    private Weather weather = new Weather();

    // Template method
    public void grow() {
        digHole();
        plantSeeds();
        mulch();
        while (! weather.frost()) {
            water();
            prune();
        }
    }

    protected void digHole() {
        System.out.println("Dig hole");
    }

    protected abstract void plantSeeds();

    protected void mulch() { }

    protected void water() {
        System.out.println("Water plant");
    }

    protected void prune() { }

    // Delegate method available to subclasses
    protected final boolean isWarmClimate() {
        return weather.isWarmClimate();
    }
}
```

```java
class Tomato extends Vegetable {
   protected void plantSeeds(){
      System.out.println("Plant tomato seeds");
   }

   protected void mulch() {
      if(isWarmClimate())
         System.out.println("Mulch around plant");
   }
}

class Pumpkin extends Vegetable {
   protected void plantSeeds(){
      System.out.println("Plant pumpkin seeds");
   }

   protected void prune() {
      System.out.println("Selectively prune new side
      shoots");
   }
}

// helper class
class Weather {
   private boolean toggle = true;

   public boolean frost() {
      toggle = !toggle;
      return toggle;
   }

   public boolean isWarmClimate() {
      return true;
   }
}

public class Runner {
   public static void main(String[] args) {
      Tomato t = new Tomato();
      t.grow();
      Pumpkin p = new Pumpkin();
      p.grow();
   }
}
```

Output:

```
Dig hole
Plant tomato seeds
Mulch around plant
Water plant
Dig hole
Plant pumpkin seeds
Water plant
Selectively prune new side shoots
```

## Discussion

A template method is often described as encapsulating an *algorithm*. Don't be misled by the term algorithm though. There are many practical applications of the Template Method design pattern where the "algorithm" is just a few lines of code.

One particular application of the Template Method design pattern that doesn't depend on an algorithm in the traditional sense is when the pattern is used as a remedy for the Call Super code smell.

A symptom of the Call Super code smell is a class with a polymorphic method that requires an overriding method to make an explicit call to the overridden method. For example, in the class definition below the comments associated with the method `harvest()` stipulate that overriding methods must call the base class implementation of `harvest()`.

```
abstract class Vegetable {
    private DateTime lastHarvest;

    // Overriding methods must call back to this
    //   method at the beginning of their
    implementation.
    public void harvest() {
        if (DateTime.Today < lastHarvest.AddDays(5))
            log("Early Harvest");
        lastHarvest = DateTime.Today;
    }
}
```

The correct functioning of the class Vegetable depends on the ability to detect early harvests. (For the purposes of this example, an early harvest is one that occurs within 5 days of the previous harvest.) A proper subclass implementation would look something like:

```
class Carrots extends Vegetable {
   public void harvest() {
      super.harvest();
      . . .
   }
}
```

Any design that relies on programmers remembering to do something should be questioned. In this case there is a better solution and that is to make harvest() a template method. To do this you would add a call in harvest() to a new method (doHarvest() in the example below) and make this new method the extension point for subclasses.

Here is the refactored solution:

```
abstract class Vegetable {
   private DateTime lastHarvest;

   // Template method
   // Subclasses wanting to extend the behavior of
   //    of harvest() should override doHarvest().
   public void harvest() {
      if (DateTime.Today < lastHarvest.AddDays(5))
         log("Early Harvest");
      lastHarvest = DateTime.Today;
      doHarvest();
   }

   // New method for subclasses to override
   protected void doHarvest() {    }
}
```

With this new design, subclasses wanting to extend the behavior of harvest() would override doHarvest() rather than harvest().

```
class Carrots extends Vegetable {
   public void doHarvest() {
      . . .
   }
}
```

The general solution applied here is more broadly applicable (i.e not just for remedying the Call Super code smell). The general solution is applicable anytime you want to exercise more control over class extensibility.

With simple inheritance a client-facing operation is made polymorphic. Subclasses can then extend or replace the behavior of the operation. The interface for clients is the same as the interface for subclasses (see Figure 76). Because subclasses can replace the behavior of the operation, the base class gives up complete control over what clients get when they call the operation through a reference to the base class (A in Figure 76).

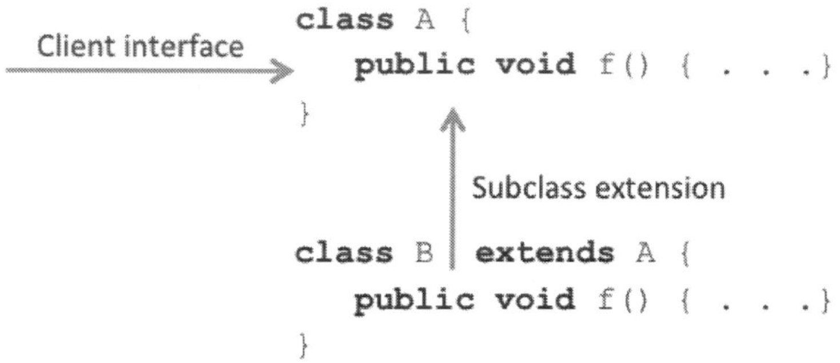

```
                         class A {
   Client interface
  ─────────────────→         public void f() { . . .}
                         }
                                      ↑
                                      │   Subclass extension
                         class B │ extends A {
                             public void f() { . . .}
                         }
```

**Figure 76  With simple inheritance, the interface for clients is same as interface for subclasses**

Sometimes you need more control over how a class is extended. In situations like this you can use the Template Method design pattern to separate the interface for clients from the interface for subclasses (see Figure 77). With this arrangement you can guarantee certain minimal behavior to clients but still allow for extension by subclasses.

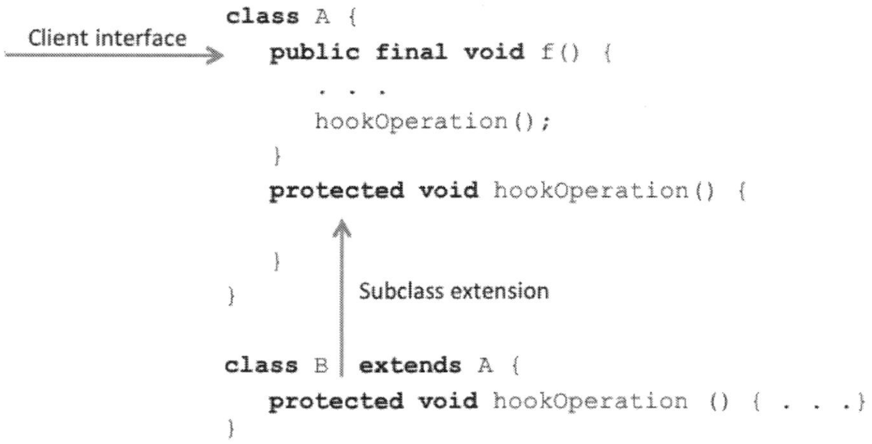

```
                     class A {
   Client interface
  ──────────────→        public final void f() {
                             . . .
                             hookOperation();
                         }
                         protected void hookOperation() {
                                  ↑
                         }        │
                     }           │  Subclass extension

                     class B │ extends A {
                         protected void hookOperation () { . . .}
                     }
```

**Figure 77  A template method allows the interface for clients to be separate from the interface for subclasses**

Something else to consider when implementing the Template Method design pattern is whether to make the template method polymorphic or non-polymorphic. In the code fragment in Figure 77 the template method f() is declared final which means subclasses are not allowed to override it. This limits the freedom to change the behavior of the class in subclasses but it also guarantees the class won't be used by subclasses in ways that weren't intended.

## Related Patterns

Template Method and Strategy solve similar problems. They both solve the problem of how to represent variations on algorithms. The main difference between the two patterns is Template Method uses inheritance to vary parts of an algorithm and Strategy uses delegation to vary the entire algorithm.

A Template Method defines an algorithm with replaceable steps. One of the steps may be a Factory Method (i.e. a method that returns an instance of an object).

# Bibliography

Alexander, Christopher. *The Timeless Way of Building.* Oxford: Oxford University Press, 1979.

Alexander, Christopher, Sara Ishikawa, and Murray Silverstein. *A Pattern Language: Towns, Buildings, Construction.* Oxford: Oxford University Press, 1977.

Beck, Kent, and Ward Cunningham. "Using Pattern Languages for Object-Oriented Programs." Tektronix Technical Report No. CR-87-43, 1987.

Buschmann, Frank, Regine Meunier, Hans Rohnert, Peter Sommerlad, and Michael Stal. *Pattern-Oriented Software Architecture: A System of Patterns.* John Wiley & Sons, 1996.

Coplien, James O. *Advanced C++ programming styles and idioms.* Reading MA: Addison-Wesley, 1992.

Fowler, Chad. *Rails Recipes: Rails 3 Edition.* Pragmatic Bookshelf, 2012.

Fowler, Martin. *Analysis Patterns: Reusable Object Models.* Addison-Wesley Object Technology Series, 1997.

Gamma, Erich, Richard Helm, Ralph Johnson, and John Vlissides. *Design Patterns: Elements of Reusable Object-Oriented Software.* Addison-Wesley Professional Computing Series, 1995.

Margolis, Michael. *Arduino Cookbook.* O'Reilly Media, 2011.

Martelli, Alex, Anna Ravenscroft, and David Ascher. *Python Cookbook.* O'Reilly, 2005.

Shaw, Mary, and David Garlan. *Software Architecture: Perspectives on an Emerging Discipline.* Prentice Hall, 1996.

Smith, Reid. "Panel on Design Methodology." *In OOPSLA '87 Addendum to the proceedings on Object-oriented programming systems, languages and applications (Addendum).* ACM Press, 1987. 91-95.

# Index

## 8

8-track tape, 47

## A

abstraction, 14, 15, 21, 117, 119
Adapter Pattern
    and Bridge Pattern, 60
    and Decorator Pattern, 61, 74
    and Facade Pattern, 60
    and Proxy Pattern, 60
    class diagram, 53, 55
    intent, 52
    introduction, 47
Alexander, Christopher, 5
Amphicar, 75
analysis model, 16
analysis patterns, 15–16
    responsible party, 15
architectural patterns, 16–17
architectural styles. *See* architectural
    patterns

## B

Beck, Kent, 7

## C

Call Super, 134
code smell
    Call Super, 134
cohesion, 39
collection object, 35
composition. *See* object composition
coupling, 2, 31, 36, 39, 56, 83, 92, 107,
    111, 119, 124
creational method, 102–3
Cunningham, Ward, 7

## D

Decorator Pattern
    and Adapter Pattern, 61, 74

    and Factory Method Pattern, 74
    and Java I/O, 22
    class diagram, 68
    intent, 67
    introduction, 63
    Java I/O, 72–74
    sequence diagram, 69
delegation, 51, 60, 63, 64, 74, 76, 86,
    119, 137
dependency inversion principle, 13
Design Patterns, 17
    Adapter Pattern, 47
    and design, ix, **20**
    benefits of, 19–22
    compared with abstract principles, 6
    compared with algorithms, 8, 19
    compared with programming idioms,
        18
    Decorator Pattern, 63
    defined, 6, **8**
    Facade Pattern, 117
    Factory Method Pattern, 93
    history of, 4–8
    intent, 22–23, 23
    Iterator Pattern, 35
    Observer Pattern, 107
    reuse, 19
    shared vocabulary, 20–21
    Singleton Pattern, 25
    State Pattern, 75
    Strategy Pattern, 85
    template, 23
    Template Method Pattern, 127
design principles, 4, 22

## E

encapsulation, 64
engineering, 2, 21
    trade-offs, 6

## F

Façade Pattern, 3
    and Adapter Pattern, 60
    intent, 119
    introduction, 117

factory class, 102
Factory Method Pattern
    and Decorator Pattern, 74
    and Iterator Pattern, 104
    class diagram, 98
    introduction, 93
fail fast iteration, 41
favor object composition over class
    inheritance. *See* object composition
File, 50, 57
FinancialTrustCCP, 93
Fowler, Martin, 16
fragile superclass, 64

**G**

Gamma, Erich, 8
Gang of Four, 8
    Gamma, Erich, 8
    Helm, Richard, 8
    Johnson, Ralph, 8
    Vlissides, John, 8
GofF. *See* Gang of Four

**H**

Helm, Richard, 8

**I**

information hiding, 36
inheritance, 52, 57, 63, 65, 75, 95, 135,
    137
intent, 22–23
Iterator Pattern
    and Factory Method Pattern, 104
    class diagram, 42
    intent, 36
    introduction, 35

**J**

Johnson, Ralph, 8
JOptionPane, 117
JTree, 49, 57

**L**

LibraryFacade, 4
linguistic determinism, 21
logging, 25
Low Sill Pattern, 5

**M**

Model-View-Controller, 20, 24, 116

**O**

object composition, 52, 63, 67
    compared with inheritance, 56–57
Observer Pattern
    class diagram, 14, 109
    example, 12–14
    intent, 108
    introduction, 107
    pull, **111**, 115
    push, **111**, 115
    sequence diagram, 110
open-closed principle, 63, 94

**P**

pattern categories, 14–18
PaymentService, 93
program to an interface, not an
    implementation, 95, 96
programming idioms, **17–18**, 103
    compared with design patterns, 18
    example, 17

**R**

RandomSample, 88
recipe. *See* programming idioms
representative sample, 88
Row Data Gateway, 125
Rule of Three, 19

**S**

sample. *See* representative sample
single responsibility principle, 37
Singleton Pattern

and multithreading, 26
class diagram, 26
compared with global variable, 25,
   **29–33**
double-checked locking, 27
intent, 26
introduction, 25
state machine, 78
State Pattern
   and Singleton Pattern, 84
   class diagram, 76
   compared with Strategy Pattern, 22,
      83
   intent, 76
   introduction, 75
static factory method, 103–4
Strategy Pattern
   and data interchange, 91
   class diagram, 87
   compared with State Pattern, 22, 83

compared with Template Method
   Pattern, 137
disadvantages, 92
intent, 86
introduction, 85
SystematicSample, 88

## T

Table Data Gateway, 125
Template Method Pattern
   compared with Strategy Pattern, 137
   intent, 129
   introduction, 127
TreeModel, 49, 57
types of patterns. *See* pattern
   categories

## V

Vlissides, John, 8

Made in the USA
Lexington, KY
20 December 2014